Praise for
Memoirs of a Counselor

"Wow! Inspiring, riveting and a book that gets at the heart of it all - the power that each of us has to heal ourselves, even in the midst of heartbreak, tragedy and adversity. Chloe Timothy speaks to the power of our inner voice to serve as our guide and our wise life-long counselor if we are quiet enough to listen. This book and the wise counselor Chloe, teaches us all how to find and listen to our own inner counselor in a profound, powerful and life-changing way. As an expert on resilience, I'm walking away with new tools not only for myself, but for those I teach."

-Kim Becking, Expert on Resilience, Best-Selling Author and International Speaker

"Simultaneously heart-pounding, heart-breaking and heart-filling, Chloe Timothy takes a troubling narrative of societal and personal oppression and abuse, and with jazz-like dexterity, she invites us to shadow her transcendent journey back to who she really is--an artist and curator of deep insight and transformational experience. She shows us both the landscape and the map for finding our way back to wholeness, and introduces us to her secret to resilience and thriving in the face of adversity: her beloved Counselor. Let the music of her words wash over you. There's healing inside."

-Kevin Anthony Johnson, PCC, Author, Executive Coach

"Life is sometimes hard, but we choose the kind of life we want to live."
"Chloe's true story is one of hope. She chooses faith in the face of unspeakable horrors. Chloe is an overcomer. Her memoirs are a blueprint for resilience and positivity. She paints vivid word pictures that are both heart-wrenching and

breathtaking. I didn't want this book to end and I cannot wait to read her next book."

-Tina Thomson, *Author, Leadership Coach, Chief Operating Officer, New York, NY*

"This book will open your eyes to new ways of looking at life and its challenges, and change your perspective on how life can be lived in a powerfully authentic, forgiving, and loving way. Through this book, we get a firsthand intimate view of the life of a wonderfully strong, courageous and humble woman who is able to overcome trials and hardship with the powerful support of a wise and loving guide, the Counselor. We all need a Counselor who makes it clear that every one of us has immense value in the world and should never give up!"

-Craig C. McCall, Psy.D., *Psychologist, Executive Coach & Leadership Consultant*

"The author writes from her life experiences and teaches us about resiliency, freedom and hope. You will be moved by this remarkable story."

-Claudette Spenst, CSW, *Editor, Social Worker*

Memoirs OF A COUNSELOR

My Life in South Africa

CHLOE TIMOTHY

© Chloe Timothy 2019

Print ISBN: 978-1-54399-047-8
eBook ISBN: 978-1-54399-048-5

All rights reserved. This book or any portion thereof may not be reproduced or used in any manner whatsoever without the express written permission of the publisher except for the use of brief quotations in a book review.

This is a non-fiction work. Real names have been used by permission. Most of the names of people, a few locations, and identifying characteristics in this memoir have been changed to protect the privacy of both the innocent and the guilty individuals. To convey the truth, I have used subtle changes in some of my experiences. All my stories are my perception of the truth.

To Ama,

You were my Grace

ACKNOWLEDGEMENTS

Thank you to my son Jethro. You inspire me to think outside of the confines of my comfortability. You relentlessly encourage me to never settle for less.

To my sister Euodias, I couldn't have written this book without your love and encouragement. You believe in me and continuously affirm me. Thank you for patiently listening to all my stories over and over again.

To my brother Eubulus, our heart-to-heart conversations are real, raw and reflective. You make me see things for what they really are.

To Gerard, thank you for your love and support. Your kindness makes me believe, and your wisdom brings balance to my life.

A special thanks to my dear friend Claudette Spenst who stood by me, and comforted me while I poured out my soul. You helped me see my worth as a woman, and affirmed me when I doubted myself. You tirelessly read through every rework of this book with accuracy, speed and love. Thank you for holding me up.

To my gifted editor, Tina Gimas, thank you for helping me tighten the storyline for continuity, and for providing insight and clarity.

Thank you to my amazing parents for understanding, and allowing me to share my story with the world. Your encouragement set me free to write from my heart, withholding nothing.

To every person who has been part of my story, I say thank you. Without you, there wouldn't be a story to tell. Every experience shaped me and made me who I am today.

Most of all, I thank Counselor for his loving kindness, constant guidance and patience in all my life's stories. I could never have survived if it wasn't for our lifelong friendship.

CONTENTS

Prologue v
1. The Counselor's Invitation 1
2. She was my Grace 21
3. His Eyes 35
4. Racism and Lost Years 49
5. It's Happening Again 67
6. The Magical World of Jazz 81
7. Smooth and Slick 97
8. A Musician's Dream 111
9. An Interrupted Dream 125
10. The Professional Emerges 143
11. For Better, For Fear 157
12. A Mattress of Roses and Thorns 171
13. The Gift Brings a Song 189
14. Death and Dying 201
15. Goodbye South Africa, Hello USA 211

PROLOGUE
Durban, South Africa 1970

It was a warm December evening. Everybody was getting ready for the spectacular Sound and Light Christmas Musical *Born a King*, produced and directed by my dad. The all-Indian cast members who had regular day jobs, couldn't wait to get together in the evenings to practice the songs for the show. Rehearsals were held in our two-bedroom flat in the city center. Excitement filled the atmosphere in our home with people rushing around, flipping of the song book pages, musicians tuning their instruments, measurements being taken for costumes, back and forth conversations about props and lighting. The list goes on.

Enthralled with the whole scene, I just sat there; a bright and happy nine-year-old girl, slightly chubby with long hair, a cute fringe and a square-shaped face. I distinctly remember the singers practicing a problematic song as my dad directed them. The tune was catchy, and the lyrics were based on a verse from the Bible found in Isaiah 9:6.

And his name shall be called Wonderful, Counselor, Mighty God, Everlasting Father, Prince of Peace.

The children sat quietly listening to the reverberation of the singers in three-part harmony. We were mesmerized. We had never seen or heard anything like it before. The more we listened to the songs, the more familiar we became with the lyrics. By the first night of the production, the children knew the words to all the songs, and we happily sang along.

That particular evening, when everyone had left, I asked my dad, "Dad, what does Counselor mean? I haven't heard that word before."

I don't remember exactly what he said, however it went something like this, "A counselor is someone you can talk to about anything, and at any time. He keeps all our secrets. He is like a very good friend."

Whatever he said, stayed with me, safely locked in my heart for another time and another place.

CHAPTER 1
The Counselor's Invitation

The light in the bedroom was dim. While my parents were away on vacation, my five-year-old brother, Jonathan, and I got to sleep on their luxury queen-sized bed instead of our bunk beds. Tucked securely under the covers, Jonathan had fallen asleep before I did. With my eyes closed, I waited to enter the fantastical place of Dreamland. As it cast its spell on me, I began to slip into the sweet rest of my beautiful dreams. Friendly faces from the stories I had read made their way into my conscious mind, evoking playful images. I entered some of the familiar scenes as a character, playing myself.

In *Snow White and the Seven Dwarfs*, I was always trying to warn her. "Snow White, don't fall for it. Half of the apple is poisonous. She's tricking you."

As Snow White takes the apple from the Queen disguised as the farmer's wife and puts it to her mouth, I cry out a second time, "Snow White, don't! Stop! Stop! Snow White!"

But she doesn't listen to me and falls to the ground. Like the previous two times, I sit at the kitchen table, tapping my fingers impatiently, waiting for the dwarfs to come home and save her.

Suddenly, the lightness of the moment gave way to the hovering darkness as my fantasy metamorphosed into a nightmare instead of a dream. A heavy hand rested on the lower part of my belly. With lightning speed, I flew back to earth, completely frozen. I must have been oblivious when he slid in next to me. Why is his hand moving downwards? A stranger I had never met before, encased with a familiar face, emerged from the darkness. Terror gripped me. I was petrified. He lifted my nightie and easily slipped his fingers under the elastic band of my little white panty covered with tiny orange daisies. I instinctively squeezed my thighs together, and immediately regretted it because I realized he knew I wasn't asleep.

"Does it feel nice, Chloe?" a familiar voice asked, as he continued to fondle me.

Now I knew it was Jimmy. I remained silent with my eyes closed, waiting for whatever this was, to end as quickly as possible. Tears ran down the sides of my face, as the invasion continued. Time seemed to stand still, forcing me to accept the unknown. Terrified to move, I let him touch me all over. Why didn't he stop? I tried desperately to say something, anything. The words remained at the back of my dry, hollow throat. Then I felt a terrible pain as he forced his fingers in me, first softly, and then harder. The terrible sensation went on and on without a word being said. I was too terrified to speak, and he was breathing hard. It was the most extended silence I have ever experienced. Muddled thoughts raced through my head searching for a logical explanation. I could feel something unfamiliar happening to my body, and I didn't understand what it was.

After what seemed like an eternity, he finally stopped. I reached my first orgasm, and I didn't even know it. With a soft, gentle voice he said, "Go to sleep. You'll sleep well now. Nobody will hurt you because I'll protect you. Sweet dreams." He turned off the side lamp and the room melted into complete darkness. He got up and left.

Now, I could hide my face. Thank God, no one saw what happened to me. Thank God, Jonathan was fast asleep. No one must see. No one must know. No one can see my shame and guilt. Why was this happening to me? Is it because I'm a bad girl? Am I being punished for something? Questions flooded my mind. I felt plagued with guilt and fear. It ate away at my heart, ripping it apart little by little. How was I to know this was an atrocity that should not have happened to a nine-year-old girl, or that what I had experienced was an absolute evil? With my face buried in the pillow, I let out a silent howl only I could hear in my head. Nobody could know what just happened. No one, not even

God! What would He think of me if He saw what happened? At that moment, a frightening thought entered my mind. If God can see everything, then He must have seen what just happened. With that realization, I turned away in embarrassment and condemnation, burying my face deeper into the darkness of my pillow soaked with tears. God saw. Maybe I could tell my father or mother, or both of them? How would I even bring myself to relate the incident? I felt so ashamed and decided I'd keep it to myself.

Darkness slowly gave way to the soft ascending light. No other night could ever compare to that night. Eyes stinging and thoughts pounding in my head, I felt my chest tighten. Soon it would be daylight, and I would have to face him. How was I going to look at his face, knowing he touched me? I wished it was dark again so I could hide in its safety. The light crawled in brighter and brighter. I heard movement in the flat. My grandmother had gotten up and was in the bathroom. I listened to every sound vibrating in my ears. Even the silence of the morning was louder than usual. Jimmy got up. I knew it because the sound came from the direction of the living room where he slept on a folding rollaway bed. There was shuffling as he folded his bedding and rolled the bed to its storage place. As I continued to track his sounds, they got louder. My heart started to beat hard in my chest. Tears longed to make their way to my eyes, but I held myself tight. I was not going to cry. I would pretend to be fast asleep, so he wouldn't know I was awake.

The moment he entered my parents' room, I knew it. The mattress caved as he propped himself in the small space between my back and the edge of the bed. Unashamedly, he slid his cold hand down my nightdress and cupped my unshaped left breast. The sickening touch of my molester stuck to me like leeches penetrating my skin. I gasped, but no sound could be heard. He knew I was awake as he continued moving his hand. What was wrong with me? Why was I feeling this way? Different parts of my body responded to his touch. I felt disgusted. I kept thinking how evil I must be. Footsteps were coming toward the room. Masterfully he slipped his hand out and stood up.

"Chloe! Jonathan! Get up! Breakfast is ready," my grandmother called before she walked to the adjacent room, affectionately known as the Small Room. "Charlee! Get up! Breakfast is ready."

All three children, one by one, slowly got out of bed. My thirteen-year-old brother, Simon, who was the oldest of the four children, walked into my parents' room. He began to chat with Jimmy about his Saturday morning plans. Jimmy was a nineteen-year-old distant cousin.

"Hey, Jimmy! Are you going to the movies today?" Simon asked.

"Why are you asking?" Jimmy asked. "Do you want to come along?"

"Yes," Simon replied, nodding his head.

"Okay, Simon. I'll let you know when I'm ready to go," he said in an almost pleasant tone. That was typical of him, always providing some entertainment or fun for everyone.

Jimmy spoke in his usual upbeat style as though nothing had happened. My skin crawled listening to his voice. This morning his voice didn't hold the safety that I had once associated with him. As I slipped out of bed, I kept my eyes on the floor and walked past him to the bathroom. "Morning, Chloe," he said. "Morning," I replied under my breath.

How was I ever going to look him in the eye again? Something had happened to me overnight. A piece of my innocence had been ripped away without my permission.

The city of Durban awoke to another day as the waves of the Indian Ocean splashed onto its shores. It was a morning like every other morning, to everyone else but me. Colorful and bright, with palm trees lining the streets, the sunny skies touched the city with a glistening aura that created a feeling of warmth, family, and friendship. Durban bustled with people making their way to the famous marketplace well known for African curios, fresh meats, and vegetables. The streets were always alive with long conversations since everybody knew somebody. It felt safe and homely with no one looking over their shoulder for any danger or threat. We lived in a block of flats, also known as an apartment building in other countries, two blocks away from the marketplace, on the tenth floor in Flat 1003.

We were Indian descendants. My great grandparents came to South Africa as indentured laborers. Life was hard in a country where racism was legalized, confining all four race groups to designated areas. We had to live in the "Indians Only" area of the city. Schools, hospitals, churches, restaurants, and beaches were segregated, which meant our neighbors, teachers, and physicians were of Indian descent. My parents, Jacob and Rachel Timothy, were prominent members of the Indian community. I had three siblings; Simon was four years older than me, while my two younger siblings Charlee and Jonathan, were seven and five years old respectively. Our two-bedroom flat had a spacious living room, a cozy kitchen, and a separate bathroom and toilet. When you entered the flat, the kitchen was located to the right, halfway down the short passageway that led to the living room. Attached to the living room was a balcony overlooking the courtyard below with beautiful views of the city. Diagonally across from the kitchen to the left, the passage continued in an L-shape. The bathroom was on the left, and next to it, the toilet. To the right was the door to my parents' room and straight ahead was the entrance to the Small Room. Both bedroom doors were adjacent to each other.

We slept in the Small Room. There were two bunk beds. Simon and I slept on the top, and Charlee and Jonathan slept on the bottom. Because my grandmother stayed with us for long periods of time, my parents installed a modern pull-down bed for Simon in the living room. He was excited because he had his space and privacy. Once he moved out of the Small Room, my grandmother slept on the bottom while Jonathan slept on the top bunk. My father ensured it was secure so that Jonathan didn't fall off while he was asleep. But that didn't matter because almost every other night he would tiptoe into my parents' room and cuddle with them.

Simon, being the eldest grandchild, on both sides of the family, was the favorite and got most of the attention. He was admired by everyone, including all the cousins, who naturally gravitated towards him. He usually hung out with the cousins closest to his age. I was either not old enough or not young enough to fit in with the groups. Feeling left out, I kept to myself and spent my time daydreaming. My dad, a high-profile businessman, traveled extensively for work and on pleasure trips with my mom. Whenever they were away, my grandmother on my mother's side came to live with us. Because she didn't have a home of her own, she divided her time between her three married children. In total, she had seventeen grandchildren. Jimmy would often stay with us while my parents were away. Everyone loved Jimmy. They treated him like a big brother. The children were usually left in his care, and he created a fun environment for them. No one knew to question Jimmy's kindness and generosity.

There were many things I had to deal with on my own. After all, I was just an innocent nine-year-old child with no idea of how the world worked. What I did know and understand was the fantastical world of daydreaming, where I could be anyone I wanted to be and do anything I wanted to do. In real life, I played with small, friendly dolls and delightful miniature tea sets. I spent hours talking to my dolls, combing their hair, or making delicious invisible tea for them. There was no one else to talk to, no one to explain to me what had happened, no one to comfort me or counsel me. One day I was in conversation with my favorite doll, Betty.

"You are so pretty, Betty, and you have such pretty hair. It's a good thing I got you as my friend. I know I can tell you anything. If I tell you what happened to me, I know you will never tell anyone. You will always keep it a secret," I said, almost waiting for her response.

That's when the realization hit me. My dolls couldn't help me because they couldn't talk. I was shattered. I couldn't talk to people about it because I was afraid and I didn't know why I was scared. Thoughts of punishment came crashing into my mind when I considered mentioning my episodic horrors to my parents. So, I said nothing. They didn't seem to notice any change in me.

Maybe it was because I was always daydreaming and my parents were usually snapping me out of my daydreams.

One morning I got up, and the bed was wet. I had no idea how it happened. Everything seemed to be going wrong, and there was nothing I could do about it. Feeling helpless and hopeless, I began to sink into a whirlpool of dread and despair. It was beyond my control, and I knew the consequences. After my siblings got off their beds, I stayed a little longer, afraid of what I would face for wetting the bed. Why was this happening to me? I couldn't figure it out. Nobody could make it stop because nobody knew what was going on with me. What I didn't realize was that I learned the art of crying and screaming silently. Slowly, I was starting to shut down. Loneliness walked into my life as a cold, friendless face. The only company I had were my thoughts. No one had access to them. I was alone. Only babies and small children pee in the bed, not nine-year-olds. This was the silent chant like a haunting melody, repetitively playing in my head the whole day. No one could hear it but me. Sooner or later, my mother would find out that I had wet the bed. It was too stressful thinking about that. On my way to school, as I looked out the window of the car, I saw happiness fade away, further and further. The distance grew wider, forming a gulf so vast that I couldn't cross over. My world had become a grey place with no lines or circles, colors, or sparkles. For the rest of the day, I sank into the abyss of my dark soul. Why had everything gone wrong all of a sudden? I had no answers. When I got home from school, my parents scolded me as expected.

"Why did you wet the bed?" my mother asked me.

"I don't know," I replied.

"How can you not know? Don't you know the last thing you do before going to bed is to go to the toilet?" she asked with an upset tone.

I just stood there and didn't answer. I knew that. I did go to the toilet before going to bed. But while I was asleep, I couldn't control my bladder.

"If you wet the bed again, you'll get a hiding from your father. Are you listening to me?"

But it happened again that night and every night after that. Every day my mother would spank me with the wooden spoon or my father would hit me with his belt. I thought to myself if I stayed awake and didn't fall asleep, then it won't happen. I tried so hard, but towards the early parts of the morning, as the dawn began to break, my tired eyes gave into fatigue. It was a losing battle. "The problem with you is that you're a stubborn child," my parents kept saying, convinced they were right in their assumptions.

I couldn't convince them otherwise. Somehow, I knew my dad and mom loved me, and I understood it was their way to discipline a child.

I heard the mocking laughter of my siblings, continuously making fun of a big girl peeing in the bed. I even listened to them relate the story to our cousins while I sat in embarrassment. Everybody in the family came to know I had wet the bed. It was around this time that I began to catch quick glimpses of a red door somewhere inside of me. I couldn't tell what it was. Wondering what it could be, I closed my eyes, trying to decipher the images. No one seemed to notice, as I faded into the shadow of my dreams.

It was Friday and the weekend was here. I dreaded Saturdays because I knew Jimmy would come to the flat. Whether I wanted to or not, I would have to face him. I didn't know if he would touch me again. And if he did, then how long will he keep torturing me? Saturday morning came, and I was still asleep. My mother and grandmother were in the kitchen. Jonathan must have been with them because he was not in his bed. Charlee was sleeping on the bottom bed below me.

A cold hand slid down my chest and came to rest on my left breast. I awoke without opening my eyes, gasping in shock and fear. Jimmy fearlessly explored my small body. I hated the almost pleasurable feeling it created, but I could do nothing about it. A strange warmth crept over certain parts of me.

My heart wanted it to stop, but my body felt a longing I couldn't understand. What was wrong with me? What was this foreboding sensation? Somehow, I knew I shouldn't be feeling this way. I felt sickened and disgusted with myself. The shapelessness of my heart was filled with pain and shame, buried in abomination and disgrace. I imagined the serpent in the Garden of Eden wrapping itself around my little body. I was entangled and trapped. Unless someone came to save me, I was doomed. Where was the prince who was supposed to rescue me? All the fairytales I had read, promised the hope of a prince who fought and overcame evil to rescue the princess, Cinderella, Sleeping Beauty, Snow White. Could anyone love me enough to fight for me and save me? Frightened and scared, I waited for someone to awaken me and tell me it was just a nightmare. But no one came.

When Monday came, I couldn't bring myself to face the students and the teachers. I thought my nakedness would somehow be uncovered. They would see what had happened. Usually, I enjoyed talking to my friends at school, especially Jess, the girl who sat next to me, and the two girls Sally and Meg who sat directly behind us. My conversations were becoming less engaged. Jess sensed something was amiss. She kept staring at me from the corner of her eye. I hardly noticed anyone anymore. There was a somber look on my face. I stopped laughing and smiling. The cheerful Chloe had disappeared and was replaced with a solemn countenance.

"Chloe, what's wrong?" she asked.

"Nothing's wrong," I replied, forcing a smile.

"But you're not the same," Sally commented as she listened to our conversation.

"I don't know what you mean," I said trying to sound like my old self, and faking it.

They were catching up with me, and I had to cover my tracks before anyone found out my secret. The shame inside intensified out of control as I began to lie and make up interesting stories about my life.

"My father is a wealthy man," I blurted out. "He owns the company across the road. He has the money to buy anything he wants." I offered the lie with pride and without coercion.

"So why do you live in a flat?" Sally asked.

"Because my parents travel overseas all the time and it's unsafe to leave my siblings and me alone in a huge house. Do you know we own many houses too?"

I couldn't help it as the ridiculous lies continued.

If I lived in a make-believe world, nothing could hurt me. Telling lies was a fascination I started to enjoy because I escaped from the world of truth, where pain existed. In my fantasy world, there was only one storyteller. That was me. I created the characters exactly how I wanted them to be. I controlled the storyline without objections from anyone. While Mrs. Naidoo, the teacher, spoke, I daydreamed.

"Chloe!" she called. Not hearing her the first time, she repeated my name,

"Chloe! I asked you a question," she said.

"I'm sorry. Can you please repeat the question?" Mrs. Naidoo seemed impatient, but I was lost in myself.

Nothing mattered to me. If I stayed in the real world, it would devour me. I had to save myself. I had to escape. It was the only way. My fantasy world consumed me. I couldn't wait to slip into daydreaming. At the end of the school day, I had no memory of what went on in my classes. My homework was always incomplete. My grades began to deteriorate. I didn't care anymore because I discovered my secret happy place. When it was bedtime, it was time for my imagination to run free in a world where anything was possible, and I could be whoever I wanted.

School became a dread. When Mrs. Naidoo asked me why I hadn't completed my homework, I lied flawlessly, "The electricity went out," or "I had diarrhea," or "We had visitors." I came up with excuse upon excuse, but then soon I ran out of them. That's when a sneaky idea entered my mind! There had to be a way to get into the teacher's good books. My mother, Rachel, had lots of pretty jewelry. If a broach went missing, there's no way anyone would know. I was becoming a treacherous little thing.

While my mom was busy in the kitchen cooking dinner, I sneaked into her bedroom, stealthily opened the wardrobe and helped myself to a broach with sparkling blue stones. Slipping it into my pocket, I walked back to the living room where my siblings were pretending to do their homework. I knew that because none of us enjoyed doing homework. They had no idea what was going on inside my naughty little mind. Looking sheepishly to see if anyone was watching, I quickly slid it into my school bag, picked up my book, and continued reading like nothing had happened. I couldn't believe the things I was capable of doing. Proudly, I felt like the *Artful Dodger* from *Oliver Twist*. My adventures in both worlds, the real and the unreal, began to inject life into my veins.

The next day, as soon as I walked into the classroom, I headed straight to Mrs. Naidoo and gave her the gift. "My mom bought this for you because I told her you're my favorite teacher," I lied without conviction.

Mrs. Naidoo smiled and accepted the gift, thanking me. She asked me to pass along a Thank You note to my mom. Happily, I took the note and said, "Okay," feeling impressed with myself. Silently I said to myself, I am a bad girl, feeling great about it and getting comfortable with it, day by day. Well, there was no way I could continue giving gifts. I had to come up with another plan.

Every day we were driven to school by Jacob, a man who worked for my father. Another sneaky idea popped into my head! What if I asked the driver to let me off at the school supply store two doors away from the school playgrounds? He wouldn't suspect a thing. Children were constantly going in and out of the school supply store.

"Driver, can you drop me off at the school supply store? I need to buy an eraser because I left mine at home." The driver suspected nothing since he could see children walking in and out of the store. When I jumped off the car, I sneakily looked around, observing who was watching. As soon as I saw that the coast was clear, I quickly hid in a corridor of a block of flats next to the store.

At 8 a.m. sharp, the school bell rang for the assembly lineup. Children started scurrying around as soon as they heard it. Some were in the school supply store, and others in the little tuck shop otherwise known as a "convenience store" right next to the school playgrounds. No one noticed me dodge and duck. I ran up a flight of stairs to the top floor of the building which led to an open roof garden. And that's where I spent the rest of my day. I couldn't recognize myself anymore. The real Chloe had retreated into some deep distant reclusive place, and a different Chloe had emerged. I was a nine-year-old girl learning how to survive in what turned out to be a cruel world. There didn't seem to be any other choice. I had to save myself from the evil people in the world. To do that, I thought I needed to be deceitful and wicked too. That way no one could hurt me again.

The second source of escape presented itself to me! One day my father called all four children, sat us down, and said, "The kindergarten teacher, Mrs. Smith, teaches piano in the afternoons. I spoke to her about giving you piano lessons. She agreed to teach you on Wednesdays after school. Lessons will start next week, which means when you come from school each of you will have to practice on the organ for ten minutes. I know we don't have a piano, but it's the same thing." At first, I didn't know what to expect, so I decided to wait and see what it was all about.

Wednesday afternoon came, and we were excited to start our musical journey.

Mrs. Smith had converted part of her home into pre-school facilities for the morning, freeing up her afternoons to teach piano lessons in the living room. Piano lessons turned out to be better than I expected. My siblings didn't have the same experience. Simon was the first one to drop out. "Dad, I don't want to go to piano lessons," he said. "The teacher is boring." My dad decided not to force him, so Simon stopped going with us.

One of the things that didn't sit well with Charlee and Jonathan was the knuckle whacking. Whenever a wrong note was played, or the rhythm was incorrect, or our fingering was messed up, Mrs. Smith whacked our knuckles with the same chopstick she used as a pointer on the music sheet. Both my younger siblings refused to go back to her. As for me, I didn't care. Desensitized and numb, I was the only child who continued piano lessons. I didn't want anyone to take music away from me. When I sat at the piano, it gave me something on which to focus. The snag, however, was that I didn't have a piano to practice. My dad decided to sell the single keyboard organ and buy a brand new double keyboard organ. It was an upgrade from what we had, even though it was more difficult to practice. I became relentless. I put all my energy into my music. This world became my second place of escape.

A deep sense of loneliness overcame me. No matter how much time I spent daydreaming, creating stories in my mind, or practicing the piano, nothing could replace talking to someone. In my solitude, I lost the ability to communicate with people and spent hours thinking of ways to continually protect myself. No one made me feel safe anymore. I learned to choose my words carefully. I learned when to speak and when to refrain from speaking, the latter being my default. I remembered my happy days with my dolls and teacups, wishing I could somehow turn back the clock, and pick up where I had left off. I remembered the squeals of delight and joy when I spoke to my dolls and played house with them. When no one was looking, I slipped back into my old imaginative world of dolls and teacups, but this time, the stories were closer to real life. I began to have intensely detailed conversations with my imaginary friends, *Oliver Twist*, *Cinderella*, and *Sleeping Beauty*, who were among the crowd.

"Cinderella, I also don't have it easy. At least we have each other," I said to her when she complained to me about her wicked stepsisters. We should ask Oliver Twist how he survived. No point in hearing Sleeping Beauty's story. "She had no idea what was going on because she was fast asleep," Cinderella told me.

I couldn't always name all the faces in my imaginary world but recognized them from stories I had read. Sometimes new faces appeared replacing old ones, after all, I manipulated the storyline because I was its creator. One particular incident stood out. It was bedtime, and I looked forward to hanging out with my imaginary friends. After kneeling down and saying my nightly prayers, I pulled back the bedcovers, slipped underneath the cool sheets before I laid my head on the pillow. I seemed to be transitioning between two worlds; the real and the imaginary, when a soft mist revealed a figure standing by my bedside. This was someone I had never encountered before.

It must be my imagination, I thought. Somehow this felt otherworldly, as a strange, ethereal feeling swept over me. The only decipherable feature was the magnetic pull of a pair of unforgettable eyes. To test the validity of the moment, I thought I'd closed my eyes, wait a while, then open them to see if the figure was still there. I was either hallucinating or daydreaming, or maybe having an experience I never had before.

When I closed my eyes, I immediately slipped into my make-believe world. I had successfully conditioned myself to escape the wicked world in which I lived. In a short period, the real world had become an evil place. Goodness had ceased to exist. My dream world was fast becoming my real world, yet I was always aware that it couldn't be real.

As I scanned the collage of faces, my gaze came to rest on the same pair of eyes I had just seen. Whoever he was, he made his way into my fantasy world. I had never seen him before, yet he looked familiar in an odd way. Drawn into the circle of his gaze, I lost the willpower to pull my eyes away. A powerful force dragged me deeper into a mysterious presence beyond the human capacity of fascination. All the other characters in my story had faded into a blur. I couldn't remember a single name of the usual people. This magnificent power began to take shape until the blur of the background was non-existent. Fiery depths beckoned me to come closer. There was no fear, no darkness, no threat, no danger.

Without thinking, I allowed myself to get lost in the sweet serenity of his overwhelming presence. His lips moved as they mouthed a soundless word, "Chloe."

The urge to run toward this beautiful creature deepened. He stood in a cloud of penetrating light with innumerable untold colors. And then it happened. He took one step forward, emerging from the light surrounding him. His face was plain and flawlessly structured. Handsome was not a word to describe him. I searched desperately for the perfect word and came up blank, for there were none to accurately characterize his features, his skin, and the shape of his face. I was captivated, and I didn't know why. Gradually, in slow motion, forms began to take distinguishable shapes, and noises turned into identifiable sounds as a glorious unfamiliar breeze whiffed through the air.

"Take my hand, Chloe," I heard him say. Without hesitation, I wrapped my small hand around his forefinger, squeezing it to see if he was real. He felt so soft and safe, so strong and secure. In that euphoric moment, I knew we were going to be friends. A thick warm liquid filled my heart, reviving cell by cell, nourishing chamber by chamber, refreshing room by room, restoring the mansions of my heart. The glorious scent of his nearness, caused me to release the trapped air of every hidden pain and grieving sorrow, pushing its way out through my lips, as my tears began to unleash themselves without inhibition or awareness. Healing waters began to flow from within as he stretched out his right hand, and placed it just below my chin. He lovingly caught each teardrop as they fell onto his palm, drop by drop. He knelt down pulling me gently into his embrace, letting me naturally and easily slip into the cushioned curve of his shoulder. A trickle of small sobs gave way to a deep dark cry coming from some unreachable place within, sounding almost unearthly when he whispered something into my ear, "My Chloe."

I belonged to someone. I belonged to Him. I was His, the One with a comforting, moving voice like a gentle stream. How could I love someone so deeply, without even knowing his name? He knew me, he knew my name, but I still didn't know who he was. I didn't want to think about that for now.

Instead, I rested in him. Through the blurriness of my tears, the sights looked undefined, unknown and unclear. Something had transpired while I was healing. I was transported to a place I had never visited before in my imagination. The more tears he collected, the clearer my vision became and the lighter I felt. The whole mix of emotions I had experienced transformed itself into a tingle of excitement. With each passing moment, the tingle grew stronger and louder. When did excitement get to have a voice?

"Everything you see has a voice," he responded. I couldn't believe he heard my thoughts. He continued,

"Yes, Chloe. I know your thoughts. I know everything about you."

Feeling more and more confident, I asked him,

"Who are you? What's your name?"

"I am Counselor," he answered. "I've been with you from the moment you were born, and I'm never going to be apart from you. No one will ever take you away from me. I will never allow them to."

Feeling sure about myself, I stretched out my right hand to shake his hand for a formal introduction.

"I'm Chloe. Pleased to meet you, Counselor," I said as he smiled at me, totally entertained by my innocence.

"The pleasure is all mine, Chloe," he responded comfortingly. "Come with me. I want to show you something."

I slipped my little hand into the safety of his grasp, and let him lead me. As we walked along a path, I happily said to myself, *Counselor is mine, and I get to keep him. He's mine. He's mine. He's mine.*

Probably tickled by my fantastic imagination, Counselor smiled to himself. He knew I had found the key to cross boundaries created by humans, breaking through natural walls and entering the celestial space through my thoughts. I found the key to communicate with him at the age of nine. I knew how to access him, and that seemed to make his day. This relationship would last throughout all the days of my life, and I didn't fully know the power I held in my grasp. I didn't realize the impact he would have on me for years to come. The bond we created together was unbreakable and rendering us inseparable eternally.

As we walked along the pathway, I happily skipped, feeling like a child once again. I'd almost forgotten I was still a child. The fog had lifted. The skies were clear and bright with not a cloud in sight. Birds were singing, and everything was alive. For the first time in what seemed forever, I heard the trees and the wind. He was right. Everything had a voice. I lifted my head to see his face and caught a glimpse of his friendly smile against the brightness of the sun, or so I thought, for it wasn't the sun, but the light radiating from him. I returned his smile. I knew without a shadow of a doubt, I could tell Counselor everything, and He would know what to say.

Counselor looks like a very wise person, I thought. *I'm sure he'll be able to answer all my questions. I'm so glad he's my friend. I'll never have to be alone again*, I thought with resolved contentment. As we walked side by side in the tranquility of the garden, I had forgotten he could read my mind.

I pondered on whether I should tell Counselor about the terrible thing that happened between Jimmy and me. Would he understand? Would he believe me? What would he think of my terrible experience? Then I suddenly remembered he could read my mind.

"Counselor, there's something I'd like to ask you," I said.

"Sure, Chloe. You can ask me anything," came his encouraging reply. During a lengthy uninterrupted silence, I realized I didn't know how to start.

"What if I think about it and you tell me what I'm thinking? Can you do that?" Without waiting for his response, I continued, "You see, I want to ask you a question, but I don't know what question to ask. Maybe you'll know the question and the answer."

Counselor knew precisely where I was going with this, but he chose to let me speak my mind. He knew I needed to vocalize the confused and unanswered emotions swirling in my little brain. This was my way of speaking out safely. Patiently, he waited for me to process my thoughts.

I stopped walking, and he followed my lead. Still holding onto his hand, I closed my eyes tightly, reluctantly replaying the horrific scene from a few weeks ago. I tried to relive every sickening moment, as the tumultuous emotions came crashing into my heart without warning. My breathing quickened as anxiety and distaste arose inside of me. Counselor didn't interrupt me although he sensed my agony. He knew I needed to go through the process, so he waited until I reached the end of the terrifying scene, before he called me back from my thoughts with a sensitivity that seemed seamless as I transitioned back into his presence.

"Chloe, I'm so sorry you had to go through that. I know how painful and confusing that must have been for you. Are you okay? Do you want to continue or should we change the subject?" he asked. He lovingly and intentionally let me lead the conversation.

"No, I'm okay Counselor because you're here with me. I want to continue. I want to understand what happened to me. Do you know if this happens to all little girls?"

"Not all little girls, Chloe. Some girls and boys have had the same experience as you. Some of them never find a way to deal with it, but you found me." He looked down at me, squeezing my little hand gently and smiled. A rush of happiness bubbled inside my heart. I was safe. Counselor was with me.

"Chloe, I know the question that you don't know you want to ask. But before I tell you what it is, I need to say something. You're a good girl, and remember to keep saying that to yourself over and over again, whenever you think about what happened. As you grow older, you'll need to keep saying it to yourself. I'll be there to remind you whenever you let me, okay?"

He waited for me to respond. Counselor knew I was battling to believe it.

After giving it some thought, I half nodded and repeated after him, "Chloe is a good girl," having a strange feeling like it could be true. He continued,

"The question you want to ask is this: Why did this bad thing happen to me?"

The Counselor's Invitation

Again, he waited for me to digest the question. I took a few moments before I said, "I think that's the question." Counselor went on,

"What was done to you, was not right. It was evil. Remember how the wicked stepmother tried to poison Snow White because she was good? This is similar. Snow White was a good girl, wasn't she?" Counselor asked, to which I nodded.

"She was good and kind, just like you are. There is good and evil in the world. Evil always wants to destroy good. Remember how the dwarfs loved her so much that they took care of her?" I nodded my head in agreement.

"Yes, they did, but I don't have anyone to take care of me."

"You have me, Chloe. I'm always going to be here for you. Even when you don't realize it, I'm right here," he said pointing to my heart.

"Also remember, not everyone is bad. There are many good people in the world. You'll find them on your journey of life. You have lots of friends who are waiting to meet you."

"Journey of life? What do you mean by that?"

"When you're on a journey, you go from place to place. Well, look at it like this: Every day is the next place. You learn new things and experience different things, some exciting, some plain, and some not-so-happy. That's how the journey is for everyone. Sometimes we stumble on new places, and sometimes we do plan to go to a new place or revisit an old place. That's how life is." He waited for me to absorb what he was saying. He knew I was getting it. I was taking it in like a sponge.

"In your life's journey, you have special gifts to make you happy, like playing the piano, and all the wonderful stories that exist in your secret imaginary world. And, there's me. I've also given you someone who loves you very much. If you look closely, you will find that person."

Excitedly, I began to scan all the people I knew in my mind. I wonder who that could be, I thought, and quickly put my hands to my mouth.

"Oops! You heard me, didn't you?"

"Yes, I did," he replied with a loving smile.

Suddenly I realized we weren't walking in the garden anymore. I was in my bed. Fascinated by the wonder of it all, I was so absorbed in our conversation that I didn't notice what the garden looked like. Sensing what was on my mind, Counselor knew he needed to bring the day to close otherwise I would relentlessly go on. He pondered for a moment before he said, "If adults had the same enthusiasm as you to learn more about themselves, the world would be a better place. If only."

Not waiting for my response, he continued, "Okay, I think it's time for you to go to sleep. When you awake, I'll be right here waiting." He knelt down and kissed my forehead, giving me a tender hug. I threw my arms around his neck and said,

"When I grow up, I want to be a counselor just like you."

"You will Chloe, you will," he smiled assuredly.

"I love you, Counselor. Goodnight."

"Goodnight, Chloe," he replied as I trailed off to sleep.

CHAPTER 2
She was my Grace

The next morning was brighter than any morning I'd ever known. As I sat up in bed, I lifted my hands above my head and stretched lazily, still feeling exhilarated from the unforgettable experience with Counselor. Then I remembered he said he would be waiting for me in the morning. Where was he? Was it a dream? I didn't know what to make of it. Closing my eyes quickly, I called his name,

"Counselor," and in the blink of an eye, he was right there, just as he promised.

"Good morning, Chloe. Did you sleep well?" he asked with a smile and a warm, welcoming voice.

"I slept like a baby," I said with a sweet satisfied tone. He seemed tickled by my response.

"So, do you remember the conversation we had last night?" he asked.

"Yes, I do. Yes, I do. Yes, I do." I sang out melodiously.

How could I ever forget? In all the stories that existed in my imaginary world, never before had I met anyone like Counselor. And the most baffling thing was that all my other friends had somehow disappeared and I didn't even miss them. I was ecstatic. I would trade all my friends just to have him.

He put his tender, loving hands on my tiny shoulders, and looked squarely into my eyes. With a deep and kind voice, he said, "I'll be with you throughout the whole day even though we won't be speaking like we are now, and like we spoke last night." Pausing for just a moment, he continued, "Always remember, I AM WITH YOU. Okay?" He waited for me to confirm that I understood what he had said.

"Okay. I'll remember." I offered happily.

With that, I got off the bed and headed to the bathroom to wash up and get ready for school. Confidently, I walked into the classroom and realized that the teacher had my full attention for the whole day. I knew Counselor was with me all the time because I could feel him. He knew that even though I believed it when he said it, I would forget it when evil showed up again. He promised he would never give up on me. He knew no matter how long it took, he would be there every time the intrusive thoughts of the past reared its ugly head.

It was Friday afternoon. I had a pretty eventful week. My conversations with Counselor deepened every day. We did so many things together; go for a walk on the beach, watch the sunset together, or go cycling along the garden path. I did stuff with Counselor I thought was impossible. He made everything in life's journey look possible. I believed I could do anything as long as he was with me, and that was enough for me. When we spoke, time stood still. As we walked on the palm tree-lined sidewalk, I felt anxiety creep up. Counselor sensed it immediately.

"What's wrong, Chloe?" he asked. I shifted nervously.

"The person who did that bad thing to me may visit tomorrow, and he may touch me again."

His heart broke as a single teardrop rolled down his face. He held my little hand tightly and turned away so I wouldn't see him crying. He wanted to be strong for me.

"If the same thing happens, tell him not to touch you. I'll be with you, but only you can say the words."

I nodded slowly and said in a low voice,

"I'll try but please don't leave me, and please don't look at what he does to me. I'll feel embarrassed."

"Never feel embarrassed with me. I love you, and I'll always see you as pure and precious because that's what you are. You're a good girl Chloe, and you're my Chloe."

We hugged each other and said goodnight as I slipped into a deep, peaceful sleep.

I was awakened by the familiar cold touch on my breast. A horrible feeling came over me as I realized it was happening again. I tried to say something as Counselor had said, but the words were stuck in my dry throat like a hard pill. The now familiar sensations were beginning to creep across my body in specific areas, and I hated it.

Chloe is a good girl. Chloe is a good girl. I kept saying it over and over in my head. I didn't want to entertain the pleasant sensations I was getting accustomed to. My eyes still closed, I tried desperately to focus on Counselor's face, but I couldn't find him. I couldn't see him because my body was screaming for attention. This was a losing battle, and there was no escape for me.

Chloe is a good girl, replayed in my mind as tears made their way through my shut eyelids and slid down the sides of my temples, dampening my hair, waiting for it to be over. Jimmy handled my body like it was a toy he owned. He didn't feel he needed permission to touch me. How bravely he explored every part of my petite little frame. When it was over, he slipped his hand out and casually said to me, "It's time to get up."

The day was miserably bleak. I was in a ghastly daze, walking and moving like a zombie with a blank stare. I stayed in the room I shared with my siblings, the Small Room for the rest of the day. A strange idea entered my mind, and I acted on it. I took the key from my wardrobe, went inside the wardrobe with the key, then pushed the lock closed from the inside, waiting for someone to come and save me. Questions raced through my mind,

Who will save me from the locked wardrobe? Who will protect me from my molester? Who will rescue me from this nightmare?

Sitting inside the wardrobe, I tried to close my eyes and concentrate on Counselor, but Jimmy's face was all I could see. I hated him. I hated myself.

"Chloe? Chloe? Where are you?" I could hear my mother calling me.

I sat silently in the dark wardrobe like a small lump. My mother's voice rose in pitch as she continued to call my name. When no reply came, she began to incessantly scream at my father to look for me. It sounded like he was getting impatient with her loud, relentless nagging. She could provoke him until he got really mad, and she would do it regularly.

"Jacob! Look and see where Chloe is hiding. She needs a good shot for being disobedient and not answering."

Huddled in the wardrobe without a sound, I wondered why they were taking so long to rescue me. I couldn't understand it. After a few seconds, I could hear my dad call my name. A note of excitement began to rise inside of me. Dad is going to save me; that was all I thought. He called my name again, and I still didn't reply. Then I softly whispered, "Please find me. Please come and look for me. Please save me, Daddy."

As I repeated these words, my dad heard soft sounds coming from the wardrobe. Seeing no key on the door, he asked,

"Chloe, where is the wardrobe key?"

"I'm holding it in my hand," I replied.

"Why are you so stupid? Why did you do that?"

I could hear him desperately trying to open the door with a tool. After a few minutes, the door swung open. Upset and impatient, he dragged me out of the wardrobe, pulled his belt out of his trouser loops, and spanked me. I couldn't believe that the person who I thought had rescued me, was now punishing me.

I began to sob from the pain inflicted on the inside and the outside. Beaten and defeated, I cried out,

"I'm sorry, Daddy. Please forgive me. I won't do that again. Please stop Daddy. Please!"

He didn't hear a word I said. My grandma ran into the room and tried to stop him, but she couldn't. Trying hard to hold his hand from swinging another shot, my grandma lost her balance as she shouted out this time,

"Jacob, what's wrong with you? Stop hitting the child."

When my father's beating came to an end, he slipped his belt back into his trouser loops and walked away without a word, followed by my grandma shouting at his back. I lifted my tear-stained face and looked at him moving farther and farther away from me.

This was not the person Counselor spoke of. It can't be him. My dad doesn't love me. Why doesn't he love me? Then who is the person Counselor spoke about? He said someone loves me very much. Who could that be? I thought sadly. I somehow expected my dad to read my mind. When I was growing up, disciplining children by beating them was part of the culture. Even schools condoned beating children. Headmasters and teachers beat children all the time. Yet I wanted my dad to defy the culture and save me without being informed. If Counselor could read my mind, then my dad should be able to read my mind as well.

I began to doubt Counselor. He promised he would never leave me. Where was he now? I couldn't see him. I couldn't feel him. I couldn't even hear him. I was alone again, but this time it felt worse. I quickly got up, went to the restroom and locked the door. Now I was safe. Now I was protected. Nobody can beat me for locking myself in the toilet. Uncontrollably I cried, as I sat on the floor of the restroom, pulling my hair to inflict pain on myself. There was pain all over, covering me like a blanket. I was sucked into an unending downward spiral not knowing where it will end. Will I ever find my way home again? Counselor was far from my mind.

Emerging from the restroom, I went to the Small Room when suddenly I was drawn to what felt like warm, sweet honey flowing lazily on my tongue, the touch of comfort like a baby in its mother's arms, and the sound of crackling wood graciously illuminating the fireplace.

Was it my imagination or was it real? It filled the room as I closed my eyes and breathed in the taste of acceptance. What was it? Thirst had drained the salty sap choking roughly in my throat. Even my watery tears lacked the power to quench my sadness. It left me wanting, needing. I felt weighed down like a rock thrown into a pond. The deafening silence came to a sudden halt as I walked straight into the great open embrace of my Grandma's arms. Peace and tranquility infused the atmosphere. She was the oasis in the middle of my burning desert. She was the honey and the comfort and the warmth. How could this force be that powerful as to dispel the contraption of darkness and despair? But it did. It did. Just sitting there, simple and sweet, unassuming, with nothing to impress the crowds. There she was. My grandma. This must have been who Counselor was referring to.

A rush of exhalation escaped my lips as my lungs began to breathe again. If only grandma knew everything that happened. She only experienced what she just witnessed. There were no words to speak of untold tales that ripped through the steel of night. It didn't matter what she knew, but that she understood. Without being informed, she was enlightened. Her soft eyes shone with insightful truths and released healing love that somehow made a way into the chambers of my infected heart. As I lifted my head and looked into the deep pools of Grandma's unconditional compassion, I hungrily drew from her strength. Gradually I regained my balance, and pulled myself together trying desperately to hide the pain. A smile penetrated the turmoil within and broke free. Although I didn't want Grandma to cry, a few teardrops rolled down her cheeks. She loved me. She was my Grace.

That was her name: Grace. A petite small built woman three inches short of five feet. She always moved with a lightness of foot. Never once had she raised her voice to an overpowering pitch. Never once had she lifted her hand to deliver punishment or pain. Never once did she turn away as if dismissive or implying rejection. There was something different about this refreshing city of hope and restoration, for that's what she was to me, a city of hope. No place delivered the transient experience of being in her presence. She had an inexplicable ability to dispel every darkness looming in the corridors of my mind. I often wondered about her unearthly beauty and what lay beyond the structure and beneath the foundation of this angelic face beaming in front of me.

With outstretched arms, she took me in her embrace like a dreamy cloak. I allowed myself to slip into the reverie of this beautiful creature. But it wasn't a dream. It was real. I felt special to belong to one such as this! The trapped air in my imploding lungs gave way to the newness of fresh air. *She was mine! She was my Grace!* was all I kept saying to myself.

"Hello, my darling! I'm always praying for you," she said as she tapped the seat next to her inviting me to sit down. I slowly sank the load of my weight into the chair, rested my head on her small shoulder, and expelled, "Ama!" It was the sigh I had waited all day to release, a sigh all her grandchildren knew so well, for that's what she was known by, Ama. Finally, I was home in the vast open room of my Ama's heart. Nothing had the power to tear me apart anymore. Nothing.

Out of the blue, a melodious string of notes floated through the air as Ama sang her favorite song, so sweetly, softly and gently. Her song penetrated my tightly wound pores and brought life to the dead wood of my heart. To me, it was a lullaby, the only one I ever knew. Ama sang it in the vernacular, and although I didn't understand a word of it, I remember the tune so well. With her lilting quivering voice, she sang to the tune of *Oh, My Darling Clementine.* Counselor was right. Someone loved me very much. I was eager to tell Counselor that it was Ama.

That night when I got to bed, I knew I would meet him. There was a strange kind of expectancy inside my stomach as it fluttered. Closing my eyes, I slipped into my world, and there He was, just as I expected. His eyes held a power that could search deep within my soul. He knew my unspoken words as though he lived inside my heart and my mind.

"I know who you were referring to. It was Ama," I said. He smiled, as he nodded. I continued, "I don't know why I didn't realize that before. I should have known it was her. I love her so much."

"I know you do, Chloe. You love your parents too, and they love you as well."

"I know they do. They do love me even though I may not feel that way at times, but I know how much they love me," I said, feeling an overwhelming sense of gratitude and love.

"Sometimes grown-ups get so stuck in their grown-up issues. They tend to forget about the most important people around them, their children. They don't mean to. It just happens."

"When I become a grown-up, I'm not going to forget my children," I said innocently. Smiling, he took my little hands in both his hands and reassuringly offered,

"And when you do forget, I'll be there to remind you." Filled with tender love, I threw my arms around his shoulders,

"Thank you, Counselor. You're my best friend," and I fell into a deep, peaceful sleep.

Ama was always reading her Bible or singing hymns as though no one was there but God. She truly loved God. All her children were raised Christian including my mom. My dad was a leader at the largest Indian church in Durban. He was always involved in church activities and events. These activities gave him a break from the erratic episodic outbursts of my mom. Mom was always highly strung and easily triggered by misinterpretation of what people were saying or not saying to her. I always heard her say to her close friends, "I'm a bag of nerves." I didn't understand what she meant by that. My mom exhibited extreme behaviors. She was loving, funny and exciting to be with, but in a split second, she became an entirely different person. Unbeknown to everyone including herself, she had a chemical imbalance. Because of the stigma attached to mental illness, no one in the community went to see a mental health professional if they experienced heavy depression. As a result, both my parents frequently argued while my siblings and I quietly sat in our room listening to the commotion coming from the main bedroom. Home wasn't always a peaceful place for me. Just when I thought everything was going smoothly, another outburst would occur.

One evening, there seemed to be a lot of commotion going on. We were asked to go to our room and stay there. Ama was our tower of strength. She'd console us and assure us all will be well. In the silence, we heard the sound of an ambulance. The more we listened, the louder it got. As it approached, fear loomed over us. We were scared. We knew something was wrong but didn't know what it was. We could hear a scrambling urgency coming from the other side of the door. Simon, my older brother, curiously cracked open the bedroom door to investigate. There were men dressed in blue uniform, pushing the stretcher toward our parents' bedroom door, frantically rushing and shoving. After a few moments, we saw our mother being rolled out on a stretcher, through the small gap in the opened door. She had overdosed. I remember thinking, *Will I see my mom again? What's going to happen to her?*

That night, Ama prayed with the four of us before bedtime. I could hear Ama praying all night for my mother, and when she stopped, she broke into singing. Her quivering voice sweetly released melancholic melodies that penetrated the freezing heart and mended the broken soul. The notes resounded in the darkness, offering comfort to our troubled minds. Every song she sang with her untrained voice, sounded like a lullaby.

My mother suffered intense depression and had overdosed numerous times. The ambulance came again and again. Each time, Ama sang her endless melodies for us. But she couldn't always be there because she had to spend time with her other grandchildren too. Whenever she left, we were confused and felt deserted, not knowing where to go if something went wrong. For me, it was yet another bad thing. I thought it was my fault. Maybe this was happening because I was a bad girl, and the family was being punished. I didn't know. I'd even forgotten about Counselor with all the drama going on. I had to do something. I had to find a way to get rid of the evil. Who was going to protect Charlee and Jonathan, my younger siblings from the vicious bite of this evil presence that had invaded our family? I felt the need to safeguard them from some obscene creature who had buried itself in the walls of our home. I had to keep a close eye on both of them. I had to be extra vigilant. I would not allow the same thing to happen to them too.

My father was usually absent, either at work or involved in some church activity, and my mother was asleep most of the time due to her anti-depressants. Simon found an escape by hanging out with either his friends or our cousins, Julia and Molly. They were closer to his age, making it easier for him to relate to them. Charlee and Jonathan ended up being in my care whenever our mother wasn't able to take care of them. What I remember fondly is my mother making breakfast every morning, fixing our lunch for school, braiding my hair, preparing a snack when we got back from school, and cooking dinner while we did our homework. My father and mother were, in all honesty, good parents, but for me, they were emotionally unavailable. Maybe I felt different from my siblings because of the evil thing that had happened to me. Maybe if I dared to share the evil situation with them, then things would have turned out differently. I didn't know. I didn't have the courage to confide in Ama, my dad or my mom about Jimmy. I felt fear whenever I thought about telling any of them. Counselor was the only one I talked to.

Always feeling the need to protect Charlee and Jonathan, I never let them out of my sight. I watched over them vigilantly. Nobody was going to touch them. Nobody!

I mourned the relationship I never had with Simon. How I wished I could have talked to him and told him everything, yet it seemed like he didn't want me hanging around him. In my mind, I felt as though he was embarrassed to be my brother. Growing up, we weren't close, and the gap grew as I approached my teenage years. I wanted Simon to accept me like he accepted Julia and Molly. I didn't feel as pretty as they were because I was fatter and shorter. It was easy to think of myself as fat, after all my nickname was Fatso. Everyone called me Fatso. I hated it so much. Before long, I began to believe it about myself, detesting the reflection in the mirror. That was the narrative I started to tell myself. There were times, I withdrew from everything and everyone, an empty shell, shedding tears no one could see. No one but Counselor. There was one time when my mom referred to me as "Fatso" in front of the whole family and everyone laughed. It was humiliating. That night I had to tell Counselor how I felt.

"Counselor, when people call me Fatso, I hate it. Why am I so fat?"

He looked at me adoringly and said, "You are perfect in my eyes. No one can tell you who you are or what you look like. The next time someone teases you, let them know you are God's special creation, and that you are fearfully and wonderfully made." I smiled. Counselor always responded with such kindness and wisdom.

There was another place under the sun I basked in, besides my imaginative world, my conversations with Counselor, and the restfulness of being with Ama. It was a place where sounds lit up my dark world, bringing resolution to the continuous dissonance of my life. I found myself at the organ, practicing. There was no pedal, so I used a book on the floor, pretending it was the sustain pedal of the piano. I forgot about the complexities of my young life. It was like a toy stuffed with thorns and stones. The flawless texture of the keys under the spell of my fingers gave meaning to the world around me. Music had a voice which spoke with a higher density and clarity than the English language. It had no bounds and no barriers, just a limitless space filled with intricacies that couldn't be understood. The timing was timeless, the tones were outside of any known dimension, and the textures produced were almost tangible. It had the power to break through systems and structures constructed in my mind, evoking the spirit within.

With much determination, I practiced the three required pieces and scales for the Grade One syllabus. I was ready to sit for my first classical piano examination. Nervous and excited, I had to refrain from pacing the floor of the waiting area. Five students of Mrs. Smith had enrolled for their exams including me. We listened to the sounds of classical music floating through the hallways, coming from the examination room.

"Chloe Timothy?" the attendant called. Raising my hand to indicate that was me, I stood up and followed the woman down the hallway to the examination room. "Wait here," the woman said.

Nervousness replaced my excitement. Because of this, my warm hands were now cold and sweaty. Then I remembered Counselor. I had lost sight of him because I was so focused on my nervousness. As it is, I already felt inadequate since I hadn't even practiced on an actual piano with a real sustain pedal. Right there while I waited, I closed my eyes, and whispered his name in my mind, "Counselor," even though no one could hear, and there he was. He took my hands in his, gave me a gentle squeeze, and suddenly something snapped in place. My eyes flew open as I looked at my hands, for they were not cold anymore and the nervousness was gone. I wasn't even anxious. I sensed an overwhelming calm.

Just then, the attendant opened the door and beckoned me. I walked in steadily, greeted the two examiners in the room, and took my seat at the piano. Closing my eyes for a moment, I said to myself, *Chloe can do this. She is a talented pianist.*

After the preliminary scales, I poised myself to play my first piece. Fingers on the keys, I adjusted my breathing and allowed myself to slip into the delightful beauty of the music, which came from my heart through my fingers. Still caught up in the magic of the moment, I played my second rendition, followed by the last piece. I brought myself back to the room after being transported by the music and opened my eyes to see the captivated looks on the examiners' faces. Standing up, I gathered my music and respectfully said, "Thank you," then walked out of the examination room. It was a blur. I wanted to replay the experience over and over again like a reverie.

A few weeks later as I entered the studio, my piano teacher smiled at me and said, "Your examination results arrived yesterday." Suddenly I was anxious. *What if I didn't do well? What if I scrapped a pass? What if I didn't get a Merit? What if....* My thoughts were interrupted by Mrs. Smith, "Congratulations Chloe! Well done!" She handed me the report. When I opened it, I couldn't believe what I saw. Distinction. I passed with distinction. I smiled a sigh of relief and ecstasy. Mrs. Smith continued,

"I'm proud of you, Chloe. You're the only student who received a Distinction."

Experiencing this accomplishment validated me in so many ways. I didn't fully understand why. It somehow made me feel valued and worthy. I said to myself, *This is mine, and no one can take it away from me.*

When I got home, I shared the news with my dad and mom. Happily, they hugged me in acknowledgment.

"Congratulations Chloe!" my Dad said.

"Now on to Grade Two!" My heart was filled with happiness. Seeing how proud my parents looked when they saw my results, made me feel even more satisfied. It turned out to be a perfect day!

CHAPTER 3

His Eyes

Still in a daze, I got ready for bed and couldn't wait to share the news with Counselor. As soon as I closed my eyes, I was transported to a breathtakingly beautiful garden. Sweet aromas of fragrance and flavors I couldn't count, dancing colors of fascinating shapes and forms, animated textures like sparkling rocks and bubbling clouds, singing flowers squealing and giggling, and rhythmically swaying branches of glistening trees, were spectacular. This untouched beauty was a world all on its own. Suddenly, an exquisitely colorful butterfly floated lightly in front of me, dancing to the orchestral arrangement of nature's sounds. This element of musical genius was beyond the capacity of anything I had heard before. Somehow, I understood the butterfly was beckoning me. I followed it until we reached the center of the garden. In front of me, suspended as the precious treasure of the garden, was a big red heart, soft and pliable. This piqued my interest. I had to know more. I had to see what lay within the big, red heart.

Curiously, I put my hand out to touch it when Counselor appeared. He found me fascinated by the sights before me. Not wanting to disturb the moment of pure ecstasy I was experiencing, he watched as I began to investigate the beautiful heart. If only I could have understood the magnanimity of this mighty organ. If only I could. Tenderly, he interrupted me,

"Fascinating, isn't it?"

"Unbelievable!" I paused for a moment before I asked,

"Counselor, what is this? It's so beautiful," not taking my eyes off the big red heart.

"That's going to be a long conversation, Chloe, and I'll tell you all about the Big Red Heart. We'll be visiting the Open Gardens very often throughout your life. Every time we're here, you will learn a little more about the Big Red Heart. But for now, I want you to enjoy the sights and sounds of this beautiful place." I was content with that for now. I could stand here all day watching the Big Red Heart, beating. Yes, it was beating. It was mesmerizing.

Then I remembered the results of my piano examination, and excitedly, I lifted my bold, beautifully bright eyes until I was looking directly into his, "I've got good news for you," I said. I proceeded to relate the story of my accomplishment. Counselor applauded me, smiling widely and clapping his hands in a celebratory cheer. Just observing his excitement for me, caused me to chuckle.

Every year I enrolled in the Royal Schools of Music piano examinations, sometimes twice a year. Music pulled me into an elevated state of reverie. My accomplishments had my name on it, and no one could ever take it away from me. That's how I was going to live from now on, exam after exam, feeling better and better about myself. My fingers danced across the piano keys with ease of mastery. It was time to learn a few hymns and choruses that I sang in church. The very first hymn I learned to play was "Beautiful Words of Life". Once I mastered it, I played it over and over, letting the simplicity of the melody wash over me as I hummed along.

Piano lessons continued. I had outgrown Mrs. Smith, and my father looked for another piano tutor. I then enrolled in a music school that not only taught piano but other instruments as well, including the organ. My lessons were split between the piano and the organ. In addition to classical music, I had the opportunity to learn pop songs. This musical genre introduced me to playful chord structures and progressions. It opened up unexpected possibilities for me as I experimented with different variations, adapting it for the piano. One day, when

I got home after school, I saw an upright piano in the living room. My dad had bought me a real piano. My heart softened. *He loves me*, I thought. I hugged my dad and thanked him before I sat down and played my very own piano for the first time in my life. I spent endless hours with my beautiful instrument.

I was fifteen when I had made my debut as a musician. I remember one particular afternoon. A pastor friend of my dad called to ask me if I would play for a mini-conference he was holding, which was a small-scale conference of about a hundred and twenty attendees. My immediate response was, "No," as fear gripped me.

Just thinking of playing in front of that many people was too daunting for me. *What if I make a mistake? What if I play the wrong chord or lose my rhythm? What if I don't keep up with the congregation?* All these thoughts went flying through my head.

"I can't do it," I told the Pastor. He assured me I would be fine.

"Chloe, all you have to do is learn to play five short choruses. The conference is two months away, and you have enough time to practice." The more he encouraged me, the more I began to believe I could do it. By the end of the conversation, it was settled. My musical performance journey had begun.

The date: September 11, 1976. I just turned fifteen, less than two weeks before. It was a huge moment for me. I remember it vividly to this day as I convinced myself, *Chloe is a talented pianist. She isn't afraid to play in front of so many people.*

Music filled the sanctuary tent, as my fingers fumbled across the keys of the Hammond organ. Eyes fixed on the sheet music in front of me, oblivious to the audience singing along, I nervously translated black notes on white lines, into something audibly familiar. It was the third evening of the four-day event, needless to say, my very first time playing in church. Sweaty palms and a rumbling tumbling feeling inside my stomach could have been signs of hunger or nervousness. I couldn't say which one it was. As I struck the final two chords in a suspended Amen, a sigh of relief escaped my lips. What an ordeal! Lowering my head, I whispered under my breath, "Thank God!" as I removed my stressed infused hands from the keys, and gently rested them on my lap.

After fully releasing the taut anxiety of performance, I lifted my eyes over one-hundred-and-twenty heads, and there standing at the back of the small tent, a stunning pair of eyes held mine, suspended in a timeless moment. It was my first love. Growing up, I had turned into a closed, introverted teenager because of the abuse I had endured. But, the pure intensity of his gaze, pierced through the thick curtain of separation and protection, captivating me. For the first time in my life, I felt a flutter in my stomach. Instinctively my right hand slid to the base of my throat. After the realization I was staring, I dragged my eyes away in embarrassment. For the rest of the service, I focused on the speaker, hearing absolutely nothing. His eyes had seared my mind with an irremovable mark, and I couldn't get it out. At the end of the meeting, I tried to scan the crowd for his face casually. He was nowhere to be seen.

On Monday afternoon, I had just gotten back from school when the phone rang. I picked it up and casually said, "Hello."

"Hello. Can I please speak to Chloe?" came from a soft male voice on the other end.

"This is Chloe. Who am I speaking to?"

"My name is Jason. I saw you on Saturday night at the event." My heart pounded loudly in my chest. I knew it was him.

After a brief conversation, he promised to call the next day. He called every day that week, and I was dizzy. In my culture, girls weren't allowed to go out with friends before marriage. All my friends had to visit me at home. That way my mother could keep an eye out.

Saturday arrived, and he was coming to visit. I didn't understand the surge of emotions awakened within me, confusing and exciting. Around 10 a.m., there was a knock on the door. There he stood peacefully, a slender man about five feet seven, handsome features on a square-shaped face, light in complexion with a soft tender smile tugging around his lips as it reached his eyes. I was tongue-tied when I saw his eyes. Pure, honest and real. How I wished I could have understood the treasure that lay beneath the tenderness then, instead of later.

"Hello, Chloe."

"Hello," I spoke in a voice softer than his.

A first of many Saturdays, for almost five years, he came faithfully. He declared his love to me every time we spoke, even though I didn't reciprocate. He never held my hand, nor did he kiss me. His love was patient and tender, deep and endless. He wanted to wait until I was ready. I had no idea how he knew I wasn't. He made every attempt to understand me. I just couldn't open my heart and let him in. We spoke for hours on end. We shared our hopes and dreams. We were special friends. Jason was my safety and my rock. Nothing I said or did would make him love me any less, but there was always just one thing hovering like a dark cloud over the relationship. He sensed it because at times I saw confusion in his eyes. I trusted Jason, yet I couldn't give him my heart. I couldn't say, I love you. Every time I tried to break through the wall inside, the unwelcome face of my molester emerged from a dark place, threateningly and without permission. I couldn't bring myself to tell Jason why, for fear that he would be disgusted with me, and I would lose him forever.

***

I loved being with my cousins. They noticed me and made me feel accepted. I felt a sense of belonging. They gave me advice about life. They spoke about boys and life in general. I learned so much about the world through their eyes, good and evil. They were allowed to go to discos with their friends. I didn't know what that was like. I had never been to a disco. I had never been on a dance floor.

My parents didn't allow my sister, Charlee, and me to attend parties. Once a month, we visited my aunt on the weekends. I looked forward to conversations with Julia and Molly. One occasion comes to mind. When Aunt Amy called Molly, she answered back with an edge for no reason. Both of them got into an argument with words flying back and forth. I sat there observing the whole scene when my mom said to my dad,

"Did you see how Chloe looked at me? I heard her saying bad things about me to Molly." Her outburst interrupted the exchange between Molly and her mom. Aunt Amy who was my Mom's older sister said,

"But Rachel, Chloe didn't say anything." The more Aunt Amy defended my actions, the more hysterical my mother got. Until everyone heard an unbelievable outburst,

"Hit her Jacob! Hit her! Can't you see that she's making me a fool? Why are you standing there doing nothing? Do something, Jacob!"

Her insistence provoked my dad. He knew he couldn't say anything to my mother, so he removed his belt and beat me in front of everyone. I just stood there and took it like I did so many times before. To me, it was one of many incidents. No one would have believed what they saw. Here was a fifteen-year-old girl standing emotionless as though she had no heart and felt no pain. In my mind, I repeated, "Chloe does not feel any pain. She feels no pain." After about six shots, a single tear slid down the side of my face. My eyes were cold. I promised myself I would never let anyone into my heart, not even Jason.

<hr />

Jason continued to visit me faithfully. Every Saturday, I got up and got dressed, waiting for his knock on the front door. He had just gotten his first job at a government agency a few months before meeting and falling in love with me. During the week, he called me from a call box at work, wanting to hear my voice and reaffirm his love for me. He made me feel alive. Nothing else mattered when I was with him. He made me feel special.

Around the same time, another not-so-good boy Max liked me. My mother suspected that something was going on when Max showed up at church every week, fearlessly and arrogantly eyeing me from across the narrow two-lane street of the church. Even though Max didn't make me feel safe, I thought he was more the type of person I deserved, and he continued to pursue me. I didn't discuss it with Jason. I was afraid I would lose him if I did.

When I switched piano tutors, the location of the music studio had also changed. Lessons were scheduled in the late afternoon. Without checking with me, my mother asked Jason to escort me to piano lessons every Thursday in case Max appeared unannounced. Without fail, after work on Thursdays, Jason walked me to my piano lessons, waited until my lesson ended, and then walked me home. This aggravated me for two reasons: My mom didn't trust me, and I felt Jason was a bodyguard at the request of my mom. My guard began to go up, and this confused Jason even more. I thought I was being treated like a child. If they knew what I'd been through, no one would treat me like a child again. To make matters worse, my father was convinced I was deceitfully seeing Max, so he beat me, asking me to promise never to see Max again. The truth is, I only had one face-to-face conversation with Max. I never loved him.

Jason was nineteen when he asked me to marry him. How could a prince marry someone stained and tainted? He was too good for me. He deserved better. If I truly loved him, I had to let him go. It was the only way. The inevitable had arrived on Saturday morning. He knocked at the door. When I opened it, I didn't see him; I saw love. It was his eyes. It was the same look I had seen for almost five years. No one had ever looked at me in that way. How was I going to break the news to him? He knew. I saw it in his eyes. His eyes always revealed the true thoughts of his heart. That day dragged on and on. I intentionally avoided being alone with him, making sure other family members were around. But especially, I avoided his eyes. I knew he was watching me. We usually sat in the living room and spoke, or if not, he was always busy assisting my father with chores around the house. Everyone in the family loved him. Even extended family members knew him well. Everyone expected Jason and I to get married.

When it was time for him to go, I walked with him to the elevator like I did every week, and said emotionlessly, "Jason, I don't want you to come back and visit me because I don't love you. I'm never going to love you. I don't want to marry you, and I can do better than you."

My words pierced his heart, like a sharpened spear. He couldn't believe what I was saying. I was not the young woman he knew so well. Startled and shocked at my words, his eyes filled up with tears, as he said, "Chloe, we were meant to be."

Adamantly I said, "No, you're wrong. We were not meant to be. I can do better than you." I was oblivious to the hurtful words making its way through my lips as they tore right through his heart. I saw him grappling with what he had just heard, and fighting for what he believed was his true love. There was no way I was going to weaken. This had to be done. I had to set him free for someone better than me. There was no other way.

"I love you, Chloe," he said heartbroken and devastated.

Hardened and determined, I repeated,

"I told you I don't want you to come back ever again because I don't love you."

With that, I turned and walked away. He never came back. That day, I lost the only man who truly loved me and accepted me. The emptiness of his irreplaceable love lived with me every day. How can I forget the eyes of my first love that have been seared into my mind? Time had proven it is an irremovable mark. To this day, I can still see his eyes like that first day, at the back of the small tent. His eyes of love have lived with me. I wished he didn't believe me. I wished he fully trusted in his love for me. I wished he had given me some time to settle my wild thoughts. I wished he would have seen beyond the brutal words I uttered. I wished he saw what lay beneath the hardness of my heart without me saying anything. I wished he had come back for me. Because now, I was indeed lost.

As soon as I got back to the flat, I headed straight for the restroom, my private haven, where I sat on the floor, huddled in a corner, pulling my knees to my chin, rocking gently. I broke down, and all my defenses broke down too. I cried silently for my lost love. I would never see him again. I'd miss his Saturday visits, his declarations of love, his soft and secure presence around me, and his eyes. How was I going to live without his eyes? I had to try. I just had to. My heart was broken, but this time, I broke it. No one else did. I felt I was finally in control of my heart. It was easier for me to break my own heart than wait for Jason to break it. This way, he would never have the opportunity to let me down or disappoint me. I had saved myself, or so I thought. Then a blinding realization hit me. I stood up and spoke up for myself. I wasn't afraid. *How was that possible? What made me speak so bravely?* I asked myself.

Another blinding realization hit me, for which I wasn't prepared; Jason made me feel safe. That's why I could say what was on my mind. He made me feel safe. The only other people who made me feel safe was Counselor and Ama. I didn't know if any man would ever make me feel safe again. I had to talk to Counselor. He would know what to say. He would help me sort through my thoughts, which seemed jumbled right now. Emotions running high, I just couldn't seem to think straight and couldn't connect with Counselor no matter how hard I tried. I was now starting to feel very alone. Although Ama was there, there were certain things I couldn't talk to her about. The generational culture gap was too large.

One day while was I resting my head on Ama's lap, as she gently stroked my hair, she asked me, "Why don't you like him, Chloe?" I shrugged my shoulders, and after a moment's silence, I answered softly and sadly, "I don't know." There was truth in that.

I didn't know because I didn't understand. I didn't know how to trust people besides Ama. Although I had trusted Jason, my trust was shaken when he listened to my mother's assumption of Max, without asking me if it was true. Maybe he was afraid of my answer, in case I said it was true.

Confused and deflated, the days went on, and I retreated further and further into my shell. I was twenty, and while girls my age, including my cousins, went on dates and had experienced their first kiss, I was stuck in the body of a nine-year-old child, powerless to get out. I felt fat, ugly and dirty, allowing these words to repeat themselves in my mind until it became my truth.

Consumed with the negative intrusive thoughts that kept making their way to the front of my mind, I stopped searching for Counselor. The harder I tried to push them away, the further I moved away from my imaginative world where Counselor lived.

After Jason stopped coming, things became worse for me. I was trapped in the web of my traumatic childhood memories until I realized, the earliest recollection of my childhood was the moment my molester invaded my world. The consistency Jason provided was not there anymore. I had no anchor anymore.

That night, I went to bed, wishing I would die. The little girl had grown up and become a woman. She looked like a woman and spoke like a woman, but remained in hibernation through seasons in and seasons out. Summertime never came because winter never left. That is my story, the sum of my parts. Every dream ended in a nightmare I could never escape, and every day started with the thought, "I wish I were dead." What was the point of life? I knew there had to be a reason for my existence. There had to be a cause. And maybe there was. Perhaps life was waiting for me to find my purpose, but I was either not searching hard enough or probably searching in the wrong places. Nothing happens for nothing because nothing can come from nothing. Life has a way of dealing cards, and the outcome of the game was determined by the choices I made with the deck in my hands.

Combined with the soft, quiet nature I possessed, and the inability to be courageous enough to speak up and stand up for myself, the writing was on the wall. There was one person with whom I was courageous enough to speak up. He was gone.

There were no more tears to shed. There was no heart to break. There were no disappointments to protect me from. I had safeguarded myself from future disasters. Loneliness was closing in faster and faster. Finally, I gave into the nothingness of life when a warm, loving and safe sensation swept over me. My senses kicked into gear, surprised at the turn of emotions. "Chloe!"

The sound of his voice released the old air trapped in my lungs, as I exhaled the weight of negativism and darkness, which had made me grow into a stunted tree, sucking the life out of me, craving to exist and destroy me. We were in the hallway entrance to the chambers of the Big Red Heart. It looked like a secret room. It was beautiful and peaceful. I lifted my eyes to gaze into Counselor's beauty and serenity. I took deep breaths as I breathed in the newness of life emanating from his eyes and his heart.

"Counselor," I whispered. Immediately I knew everything was going to be alright. Savoring the moment of utter sweetness, I waited a few minutes before I asked,

"Where were you when I needed you. Where were you?" He took a moment before he responded, looking deeply into the pools of my eyes,

"When you allow your paralyzing emotions and negative thoughts to consume you, then you won't be able to see. When you allow them to take up space in your thoughts and your heart, there's no place for me to restore you. The moment you let go and relinquish the right to your pain, that's the moment I can step in and do what I need to do to breathe life back into you."

He hesitated a moment and then continued.

"I can't guide and lead you when all you can think about is escaping from your pain because then your pain guides you. You cease to hear me and see me. I am your Counselor. Any decision you make without my counsel has consequences. I understand the voice of your emotions are loud and powerful. I know how you feel and how you think. This is a lifelong journey, and you will get better at dealing with it. But for now, let me take you to a special room." Willingly, I took his outstretched hand, and let him lead me.

"What room is this, Counselor?" I asked.

"This room holds countless gifts with the same name. They are all named Grace."

Looking a little bewildered, I said, "But that's my Ama's name!"

"Yes, it's your room, and all these are your gifts, Chloe. Throughout your life, you will receive them, one by one."

"Can I open the packages and see what's inside?"

"Every gift has a date on it. If you open it before it matures, you won't understand what it is and how it serves you. When you open it at the appointed time of your life, then only will you enjoy the full benefits of it."

Although I had a thousand questions running through my head, as we left the Grace Room and I walked down the corridor of what looked like a vault. Intrigued with exquisite artistry on the walls, the ceilings, and the floors, I took in the wonder of it all, utterly speechless until we came to a closed door.

"Chloe, what lies behind this door may not be what you're expecting. Keep an open mind and trust me. Will you do that?" he offered with an unusual tone which was both comforting but alarming.

I sensed something I may not like, but I trusted Counselor wholeheartedly.

"All the doors will only open if you place your hand on it, and wait until your heartbeat and my heartbeat are in total sync." He pointed to my heart and then his. He paused for a moment.

"Now close your eyes, and listen to your heartbeat." He gave me some space to bring my awareness to my heartbeat before he proceeded.

"Once you can hear yours, listen for mine." Again, he paused. "Sometimes they will be in complete sync, and sometimes not. If it's not, then wait until they align. Think about a combination lock. It works the same way. When both heartbeats click, the lock is opened."

There was silence as I waited to hear my heartbeat first. Once I identified mine, I listened for Counselor's heartbeat. It was almost in sync. Steadily, both heartbeats made their way to each other as if each had a life of its own. Then I heard for the click. I knew we were in complete sync because the door before me opened.

We entered a dark room. I couldn't see or hear anything. I grabbed onto Counselor's hand because I didn't know if I would trip over anything. I took a small step, fully alert, and waited. Nothing happened. I took another step and waited, still nothing happened.

"This is the room of blind faith, the Dark Room," I heard Counselor's voice in the darkness. He went on,

"Whenever you can't see things clearly in life, all that's left to trust is what your natural eye can't see. Your hearing becomes heightened because you can't. You have to depend on what you hear and what you sense. You have to trust your gut and believe in yourself. That's what hope is. If you don't believe in yourself, then the darkness will overtake you. A defeatist attitude won't remove it, but will thicken it, increasing the weight you have to bear."

I listened intently as he spoke, and realized that I heard every word, every tone, every sound, and every emotion because my hearing was heightened in the darkness. He continued, "This room is where you grow and develop into the fullness of your existence. The darkness makes you develop faster than the light. Think about it like photographs. They can only be developed in a dark room. The images and colors develop as they come to life. Your true image is developed and revealed in your dark room. Think about a seed that is planted in the ground. It begins to germinate in a dark place until it has the strength to push through the darkness as a green shoot, ready to spring to life and the light. This is that room, Chloe, your Dark Room. And you know that Chloe means a green shoot." He paused there and waited for my response. I was taking it all in. There was so much more to life than what I had thought.

"Do you have any questions you want to ask me?" He waited for my response.

He didn't want to rush me. This was a lot for me to absorb. Deeply pensive and utterly fascinated, I said,

"No, not yet. There's a lot to think about and reflect upon." He then presented me with the first challenge of blind faith now so I would understand the thinking behind it.

"Are you ready to take your first step of faith?" he asked.

"You mean right now, Counselor?" I asked not sure if I heard him correctly in the darkness. Immediately, I knew I hadn't trusted my hearing and sensing by the simple response I gave him.

"I see what you mean," I conceded. Another moment of truth.

"I just said I 'see' what you mean." He smiled as a soft dim light began to illuminate the room, revealing a bubbling brook with glistening fish gliding over the ripples carrying them along. I hadn't even heard the sounds of the brook and fish in the darkness. How fascinating!

"The more you learn to listen, the more you will hear. The quantity and quality of the sounds are dependent on the depth of your ability to tune into the darkness. When you can see in the darkness, nothing will be hidden from you."

As we walked out of the Dark Room, along the corridors of this magnificent structure, we found ourselves in the Open Gardens. "So beautiful," I said out loud, lingering in the incredible beauty of it all. With a tone that indicated a concealed excitement, Counselor said,

"Turn around Chloe. See what's behind you." I spun around and was in revelatory amazement. Before me, stood the Big Red Heart. Beating! We had just emerged from the Big Red Heart. I gasped! In complete disbelief, I looked at him questioningly.

"Is that my heart?" He looked at me with the purest, kindest eyes of love and care, brushing breezily over me before he answered, "Yes, it is!"

Giving me time to absorb the incredible intensity of this new revelation, he waited before uncovering another truth.

"And do you know what else?" Seeing I was hungry for more, he offered the full truth.

"What you've seen and experienced; the Open Gardens, the Big Red Heart and the chambers inside the Big Red Heart." He paused for a quick moment, while motioning his hand in a complete circle.

"This is all inside your Heart, and your heart is inside of you. Yet, you live inside your heart."

My eyes widened in astonishment. Putting both my hands on my heart, I said,

"Then I'm finally home where I belong."

CHAPTER 4
Racism and Lost Years

South Africa, home to the famous Big Five game animals, was originally a four-province country that was now divided into nine provinces. It's located on the southern-most tip of Africa, where the warm waters of the Indian Ocean on the east meet the cold waters of the Atlantic Ocean on the west. Ruled and governed by the white man, non-white races made up of Indians, Coloreds, and Blacks were discriminated against until the abolishment of the apartheid legislation in 1991. The country held its first democratic elections in 1994, electing Nelson Mandela, affectionately known as Madiba, as the first black President of South Africa.

Being a British colony, many of the customs adopted by the people of the land is of English influence, including simple luxuries like high tea and scones. South Africans love drinking tea, often sipping tea in the afternoon with a piece of cake. Around 3 p.m. without fail, my mom would call out, "Chloe, make some tea, and see what cakes are in the cake tin." I had a reputation with family and friends for making the best cup of tea. Five Roses tea with boiled milk; that's the way we drank tea.

Kwa-Zulu Natal, a province formally known as Natal during the apartheid era, has the largest Indian population in the country. Although Pietermaritzburg is the capital of Natal, Durban is well-known for being the busiest port in South Africa, and for having a stretch of beautiful, palm tree-lined, subtropical beaches, known as The Golden Mile.

West Street, the main street of Durban, with its affordable luxury stores and clean sidewalks, always felt safe to walk along, especially during the summer month of December, when the lamp poles were brightly decorated with Christmas lights and figurines while Christmas carols floated in the air. During the evenings when the stores were closed, you could find West Street bustling with families strolling along, window shopping, ice-cream vans playing carousel tunes with a queue of people waiting to swirl their tongues around soft serve in cones. Simon was usually the first to ask,

"Dad, please buy us some ice-cream." He always treated us, just so he could see the smiles of delight on our faces.

Against the backdrop of magical lights sprawling across four complete blocks ending at City Hall, people sang, "Chestnuts roasting on an open fire...," without understanding the meaning of the lyrics, yet welcomed the miraculous spirit of the Christmas season.

There was so much happiness all around. At this time of the year, people drank excessively and became rowdy. This sometimes led to swearing and ending in violence.

One December evening, my dad took us for a drive down West Street at a cruise speed of fifteen kilometers per hour. Wide-eyed and in total amazement, our gaze lingered on every decorative light and figurine. Running wildly across the road was a screaming young woman carrying her baby. She was being chased by her intoxicated husband armed with a knife, spitting abusive language and threats. Afraid to be caught in the crossfire, people scurried away from the scene. Dad swerved the car and brought it to a standstill. Jumping out of the car, he shouted out,

"Lock the doors and pull up the windows, now."

Frantically we obeyed, while my mom raising her voice, called out,

"Jacob, what are you doing? Please come back. That man has a knife." My dad couldn't hear her. His focus was on the danger in front of him. Running at high speed, he caught up with the man, grabbed him and pinned him to the ground as the police sirens got closer.

In the meantime, we were in the car screaming, "Daddy! Daddy! Daddy!" wondering if our dad was going to get stabbed. But my fearless father, strong and courageous, held the man down until the police emerged and arrested him. Dad then went over to check if the woman was okay. She was shaking with hysteria and sobbing uncontrollably. He waited until the police had the situation under control before he made his way back to the car.

Dad was the hero of the moment, and I was so proud of him. That was typical of him; rescuing people, lending a hand, providing shelter, and looking after the poor. Dad was benevolent and bighearted in nature. Every year he donated clothes to hundreds of orphans in India. He was not one to stand aside and watch things happen. He made so many dreams come true for so many people.

We lived on Queen Street, four blocks north of West Street, in the Indian area of the city. Grey Street was the main street where mostly Indian people shopped. On rare occasions, you would find a white person walking down the street. When this happened, all the Indian folk would turn and look, observing their mannerisms so they could learn the ways of the white man. Indians treated Whites with respect, even bowing slightly in acknowledgment, changing their accent to sound white, and serving them first if they entered a store. In the meantime, a handful of Indians were becoming more aware of their subservience, and gradually began to rebel, passively at first; otherwise, you could be thrown in jail.

During the year, especially over weekends, people loved to hang out on the beachfront located at the end of West Street, where the salty taste of the ocean could be felt on your tongue, and during the summer months as the sticky humidity of Durban clung to your skin. Peals of laughter and screams of hysteria rippled through the air as people tested their fear threshold with the rides at the Funfair, while others played Carnival games so they could win a teddy bear or any gift for that matter.

Two miles along the beach was another common hangout, fondly referred to as Blue Lagoon, home of the famous take-out, 'Coconut Grove.' On Friday and Saturday nights, the whole area came alive as crowds of Indians flocked, taking up every possible piece of ground, causing the place to be 'chock-a-block,' a colloquial way to say 'jam-packed.' Cars were parked everywhere, with their doors wide open, trunks popped up, music playing on the radio, meat 'braaing' which was a South African way to say barbecuing on the fire. Guys and girls were making out, others playing putt-putt, while laughter and excitement filled the air. As people joined, you could hear them greet each other affectionately, using Durban Indian slang,

"Howzit Bru," followed by the response,

"Lucker man," which means everything's good.

The Indian community shared the same facilities irrespective of religious differences, except for worship centers. Because I was a Christian, I knew hundreds of people in the Christian community. Being the only Indian female to play the organ in one of the largest Indian churches in the city, I was pretty well-known. If people didn't know my name, they definitely knew my face. I played at weddings and funerals of people I didn't even know and received my first check for services rendered. I was thrilled at the opportunities to use my musical gift! This encouraged me to start giving piano lessons at home on Saturday mornings, at the very affordable rate of ten rands per half hour. By the end of the year, I had grown my little business to ten students.

Music was becoming the world I lived in most of the time. In addition to being the resident organist of the church after my predecessor resigned, I was offered two positions at the Sunday school as a pianist and a third-grade teacher, enthusiastically accepting both.

My piano lessons continued, intensifying my practice, as I progressed to Advanced Levels. I spent hours at the piano, completely absorbed in the complexities of pieces across multiple time periods, from *Baroque* to twentieth-century works. The intricacies of musical structure and compositional techniques held my full attention. Driven without end, I picked up the guitar. Following a teach-yourself-book, I learned how to strum across its six strings, one chord per week. Before long, I was invited to play the guitar at home group meetings.

Everyone thought this was going to be my career, but my aspirations reached into presumably unexpected fields; I wanted to become a surgeon. It was the first moment I stepped into a hospital. My heart was so moved with compassion. I knew then that I wanted to be a doctor. When I got home that day, I said to my dad,

"I don't know why, but when I saw all those sick people, I wanted to cry. I wanted them to get better." With a gentle tone, he replied,

"You have a compassionate heart. The next time you see someone who is sick and feel the same way, take a moment to offer a prayer for them."

"I will, Dad," I said, smiling.

A friend of my parents who was a principal of a school convinced them that I should pursue a career in music, based on my accomplishments as a pianist. On his recommendation, my parents insisted I study music. What upset me most was that they allowed someone else to choose my career. Although I loved music, it wasn't what I wanted to do. All I wanted was to heal people. By forcing me to enroll in the Undergraduate Music program at the University of Durban-Westville, the only non-white university in Durban, my parents decided the career path for me. I wished I could have stood up to them and followed my heart. Life would have certainly fulfilled my aching heart.

Growing up in the South African Indian culture, as long as you remained single, you were required to stay at your parents' home. It was considered a disgrace for single women to live on their own while at university. As a result, I continued to live with my parents but with limited supervision for the first time in my life. Unlike high school, university required a whole new way of thinking. My schedule had huge pockets of free time between classes whereas in high school, classes were back to back. In addition to this shift in mindset, I wasn't confined to wearing a school uniform five days a week. I got to stand in front of my closet and choose an outfit to wear. What a treat that was! I experimented with different styles and colors, mixing and matching until I settled for my unique interpretation of fashion.

Unsure what to do with the empty spaces of time in my schedule, I began hanging out in the cafeteria or chatting in the corridors with fellow musicians I felt comfortable with. I indulged myself in this newfound freedom increasing my anticipation for the unknown. Everything I experienced was a wonderful surprise as I learned about the larger world around me, moving further away from the protective space I had grown in. The privilege to socialize with whomever I wanted was a big deal for me, given my introverted nature and sheltered life.

I had one thing in my favor: Besides being one of three pianists in the Music Department, I was the only one who could pick up any tune and play it fluently by ear. My keen musical sense led to my role as the designated pianist for the musicals produced by the Music Department, including the productions taken on the road. It was an exciting and disturbing time, all at once. The reason being, the constant apartheid boycotts led by the student body on the campus. Because I feared being excluded for saying the wrong thing, although I had strong convictions, I was a passive activist. During one of the police raids, I was among the crowds raising my fist in solidarity as half of us called out, "Amandla" while the other half responded, "Awethu," which means Power to the People.

The resonance of the cries for freedom echoed in the air as it circled back deep into the souls of the protestors. Advancing like a thick, dark, dense cloud was a mass of black and white policemen dressed in gravely grayish black, bulletproof gear, and wearing hard face masks. They charged toward the student protestors, opening fire and spraying tear-gas. In the midst of reverberating gunshots, smells of burning metal and crowds screaming, all I could hear spinning circles around my head was, "Run! Run! Hide! Cover!"

Panicking, my friends and I ran blindly through the smoke, the smog, and the sound of danger, hoping we could escape the whizzing bullets. Breaking into a cold sweat and gripped by fear, I frantically looked for a safe place to hide until I stumbled into one of the smaller lecture rooms where I hid under a desk in dead silence, waiting for the commotion to end. The deafening sound of guns blocked out the voice of Counselor. I tried my best to talk myself out of fear, *You're safe. You're safe. Nothing can hurt you. Just breathe Chloe, just breathe.*

Ears fully alert, I listened as the subsiding chaos surrendered to a chilling silence. Cautiously, I emerged, looking around to see if it was safe to resurface.

Experiencing the onslaught of the police force was a regular occurrence on campus. My first two years at university were an adventure: Enlightening, frightful, and insightful, all at the same time. While I enjoyed every moment of personal freedom, I came to grips with the oppression and the racial tension existing in the land of my birth. It was the first time I stood face to face with the struggle for freedom and equality. Every day crowds of students would gather either in the auditorium or the cafeteria, led by fearless leaders who addressed the crowds,

"How long will you stand for inequality?"

"Are you going to let the white man tell you and your family what to do and where to go?"

"Who's ready to join the protest?"

The provocative questions aroused the students to respond with militant shouts, "Biko! Biko! Biko!"

"Viva Mandela! Viva!"

"Free the ANC!"

All across the country, non-whites were being discriminated against. Some citizens were willing to die for South Africa, while others were too afraid to speak up. My heart ached for my country and for those who suffered at the hand of our oppressors. More than twenty years, I had lived a life protected from the harsh realities of issues people faced on a daily basis. Yet inside my protective capsule, I was violated. Do people have the power to protect themselves when there is so much evil in the world? I wanted to believe we could, but my life story informed me differently.

I wondered how many people walked around the campus like I did, with an untold tale of despair and hopelessness. My heart ached for those who were victims just like me, suffering at the hand of their perpetrator, physically, mentally and emotionally. I wondered how many stories were waiting to be told and how many stories would never be told. I could feel my heart heavy with grief for others, realizing I could be one of many victims, walking the streets of cities while others were oblivious to the invisible cloak of pain they wore to cover their shame.

It was towards the end of my second year, just before my final examinations, when I fell sick. One morning, I got up with an unbearable piercing pain on my side. Dragging myself to the restroom, I was unable to urinate, which aggravated my agonizing discomfort. When my parents saw me in this state, they rushed me to the doctor's office two blocks away. After examining me, Dr. Khan the physician, immediately referred me to a specialist. Multiple tests were run. I thought the day would never come to an end. Finally, something showed up on the X-rays. A logged jagged renal stone was causing a backup in my left kidney. When my parents heard the diagnosis, they tried to remain calm, hiding their concern so I could be brave.

"I have to admit Chloe to hospital for emergency surgery in the morning," Dr. Khan said.

"Am I going to die?" I asked, as my fears started to gradually escalate.

"No, Chloe, but if we don't operate immediately, it could endanger your life." His voice was laced with kindness.

Unable to contain the high-pressure buildup any longer, the walls of my inner dam broke with crashing momentum as I burst into tears, turning the whole day into a blur. Everything was fine the night before. How could so much have taken place within so few hours? This series of unexpected events hurled me into an unending downward spiral. Disorientated, confused and scared, I asked myself, *Why is life creating unnecessary obstacles and throwing me in unavoidable circumstances?*

Early the next morning, as the nurse rolled me down the corridor towards the double doors of the theater, I knew I had to see Counselor before I went in. He was my beacon, my unwavering constant. If I could draw from the resource of his anchoring strength, I would feel less lost and more grounded. My vessel was afloat on unchartered territory without a guiding compass to bring me to the shores of resolve. I needed my North Star. I needed my Captain. I needed Counselor.

As if hearing my request for a solitary moment with Counselor, the nurse instinctively maneuvered my stretcher alongside the walls with high windows overlooking the garden, and walked away. I closed my eyes tightly, and whispered his name, "Counselor."

With rising hope, a familiar and safely warm sensation came over me. I was immediately transported to a beautiful room colored in a myriad of white hues. Everything it contained was soft and cozy, even the gentle breeze brushing perfectly across my face. Counselor was standing in front of me with such a sense of profound peace. He took both my hands in his hands, gently squeezed it, and looked down at me with tender compassion in his eyes. His grip was secure and firm. Even if he didn't say anything, by him holding my hands, I sensed the transfusion of his anchoring strength into my weakened bones.

"I'm with you, Chloe. I'll never leave you. I'm always right here," he reassured me before tenderly stroking my cheek with the back of his hand. Sweet tranquility slowly saturated me like a gentle stream as I fell into a deep sleep.

When I awoke, I was back in the ward. Still drowsy from the anesthesia, I tried to get up and walk over to the restroom, but collapsed on the floor next to the bed. As I regained consciousness, I found the nurse helping me get onto the bed. Holding my hand gently, she said,

"My dear, if you need help, please ring the bell," pointing to it.

"There's no need to get off the bed. You have a urine bag attached right here," pointing to my back on the left side, "And you have a catheter, so you don't need to go to the restroom. Okay?"

Hearing this information without understanding what it meant gave me a feeling of helplessness and hopelessness. I didn't have the physical and emotional strength to respond, so I succumbed as my eyelids, still heavy from the anesthesia, pulled me back into a deep sleep.

By the time I awoke, the anesthesia had worn out, causing me to experience the intensity of the throbbing pain to an unbelievably numbing dullness. After morphine was administered, I settled down to a dreamy state of temporary ease. When Dr. Khan made his rounds, he explained everything to me with simplicity and kindness, quelling my doubts and replacing them with a sense of relief. The two long weeks spent in the hospital felt like two lifetimes. Every day seemed as long as a year, and every minute seemed as long as a day. In my weakened state, I lay on the hospital bed soaked with urine, constantly breathing in the clinical odor that charged the atmosphere.

Viruses and bacteria like atoms waging war in the unseen world sort to attach themselves to their victims. The patients were oblivious and vulnerable, waiting patiently to be released from the captivity of medical staff armed in white uniforms. The only sound you could hear echoing in the hospital corridors at night were squeaking rubber soles. This was far from the exciting life at university, now a distant memory. I began to wonder if it was even real.

After what seemed like an eternity, the incision had finally healed, and I was discharged. Ecstatic to return home after an overextended tiring journey, I breathed a sigh of relief exhaling the disinfectant smell of the ward. The only thing that consumed my thoughts was the excitement of university life awaiting me. Anxious and restless, I made up my mind to chase after the winds of adventure and return to university, disregarding the warning bells ringing in my head and refusing to heed the advice of my parents,

"Chloe, it's too soon to go back to University," my father advised. "Give yourself a chance to heal."

"I'm strong enough, and I know how I feel," I retorted.

"Well, don't say I didn't warn you. If you feel you're ready, then go back. It's your choice," he conceded and walked away.

The following Monday morning, I got up and realized the wind of adventure was mighty slow when I couldn't move fast enough to get dressed. Adamantly, I thought to myself, *I can do this*. Fortified, I made my way to university with great anticipation.

What started on a high didn't stay there for too long. Before the day was over, I had slowed down to a snail's pace, while the pain began to pick up speed. On my way home, I felt every bump in the road. I recalled my parents' advice. I remembered the warning bells. I had tried to run before I could walk. How foolish and unrealistic I had been! Drained of all my energy, as soon as I got back home, I gave myself over to the soft snug feel of my bed as it hugged me comfortably.

I need to rest. I need to relax. I need to sleep. I said in short, breathless gasps. After a short rest, I tried to stand up, but my soles were covered with huge lumps, making it impossible to place my feet on the floor. Overcome with concern, my father called an ambulance. Within minutes, I was back at the hospital. I couldn't believe what was happening. This was a nightmare, and I couldn't wake up from it!

On arrival, I kept slipping in and out of consciousness and was immediately put on a drip. Once I stabilized, the surgeon came by and informed me that I had an allergic reaction to the anesthesia.

Well, I said to myself, *What a story I will live to tell my children. Why wait to experience an adventure at University only? My life is already full of adventure.*

It was a turning point. I was sick and tired of accepting defeat. I made the decision to be positive and gave myself permission to be happy.

In the evening when my parents visited, I told them to bring my guitar the next time they come to visit. Sickness was definitely not a friend, and it was desperately trying to keep me down. I had to do something. I had to keep moving. I had to rise up. I had to choose to live positively. Counselor said music was my life source. His words came flashing on the screen of my mind,

"When you allow your paralyzing emotions and negative thoughts to consume you, then you won't be able to see. When you allow them to take up space in your thoughts and your heart, there's no place for me to restore you."

It was time to turn the ship around. The very next day I declared it a new day. I picked up my guitar and strummed the first chord, feeling exhilarated by the power of music and allowing its healing properties to penetrate my soul. The rest of the week was spent playing my guitar and singing songs, serenading the patients and the medical staff in the ward. Everyone loved my music. They welcomed my pleasant disposition. Soon everyone knew me by name. The soothing music gave them a break from their sickness and released them from the anxiety attached to it, even if just for a few moments. Putting a smile on someone's face made me feel better.

"Chloe, can you play *Sounds of Silence?*"

"Chloe, please sing *Sweet Caroline.*"

"Chloe, do you know how to play *Blowing in the Wind?*"

The song requests kept on coming. When the surgeon made his daily rounds, he found me sitting up in bed, singing and playing the guitar, with everyone in the ward listening to the music as it filled the place. Some of the patients who were familiar with the lyrics sang along:

The answer my friend is blowing in the wind

The answer is blowing in the wind.

Dr. Khan smiled as he witnessed the magic of the moment. He had never before experienced a patient bring the gift of music into a hospital room. Instead of the sickly smell associated with hospitals, my ward had a surge of hope and life. Patients began to feel better as their spirits lifted. They started to recover rapidly. Dr. Khan thanked me for sharing my gift of music.

"I have a gift for you Chloe," he said.

"What is it, Dr. Khan?" I asked curiously, surprised by his words.

"I know it hasn't been easy for you with the complications of the surgery and then dealing with an unexpected setback. I admire your strength and your courage. When I see the smiling faces of the patients in this ward, I'm inspired, and it's because of the joy you give to them through your music."

I smiled at him shyly, not comfortable receiving compliments or acknowledgments, and still wondering where he was going with this. He continued, "I've decided to waive all consultation and surgery fees. And when you get home, all the aftercare costs and office visits will always be free for you."

I was stunned. This surgery would have cost my dad thousands of rands, and not once did I stop to think about how he would settle the bill.

"Thank you, Dr. Khan. I don't know what to say."

"Promise me you'll always use your gift to bring healing to people's hearts."

He waited for my response.

"I promise I will," I said, placing both my hands on my heart.

And so, Dr. Khan felt it was finally time for me to go home. I wondered if this was the reason I got sick. I may not have pursued my career as a doctor, but I found a way to use my gift of music to do the same thing in a different way. Instead of healing bodies, I was healing hearts and giving the gift of hope just like the way Counselor was healing mine.

Glad this ordeal was finally over, strangely I sensed sadness creep in. I had missed my final practical examinations, and that would put me back a whole year. To progress to the next year, I had to pass the practical exam. It was one of the requirements for the Music degree program. By default, I had failed because of my physical inability to prepare for the examinations. Feeling despondent and demotivated, I was forced to repeat my second year. Disillusionment caused me to lose interest in my music studies. My fellow classmates had progressed to the next level while I remained in the same class with first-year students from the previous year. It was humiliating for me. I had lost my edge and the excitement I experienced in the first two years. I didn't care about my classes, and I hardly practiced my piano.

That year I studied less and socialized more. It was the only way to keep sane. I barely made it through my second attempt at the second year. A new set of friends emerged, a few years younger than me. That's when I met Jackie and Jerome, two people who would remain lifelong friends.

During the same year, a woodwind teacher joined the music faculty, offering clarinet and flute lessons. I decided to take up the clarinet as a second instrument since my father was a clarinetist and he owned one. It was fascinating learning another instrument. By the end of the year, the students were good enough to form a ragtime band led by Mr. Miller, the woodwind teacher. Things were starting to pick up for me. I was getting my groove back. Band practice became the highlight of my week for two reasons; I loved playing in the band, and I got to hang out with Jackie and Jerome. Jackie, a tall slim Indian girl with short hair and a playful smile, also played clarinet. Jerome was a slender Indian guy, average height, with a friendly disposition. He played the flute. He was everybody's friend.

The band sounded more cohesive and more in tune every day. Because I had perfect pitch, any instrument that sounded off-key grated on my nerves causing me to grind teeth in agitation. It took a year for the band to progress to performance level. At one of the practice sessions, bandmaster Miller made a startling announcement,

"Everyone, settle down. I have fantastic news for you." He smiled and waited until he had our full attention.

"We're scheduled to perform at Expo 85, a large event taking place in the city conference center over the Winter break."

Shouts of delight and excitement filled the band room at the incredible news. Our university ragtime band was going on the road, performing in front of hundreds of people. What a big deal! It was an opportunity of a lifetime. The rest of the day was a series of happy blurs for the band members because that's all we could talk about. Going forward, we had extra practice sessions to prepare for the event. Miller chose a repertoire of Scott Joplin tunes with some jazz standards.

Expo 85 stretched over a few weeks during the mild winter season. Bands from all around the city performed from 10 a.m. until 10 p.m. every day. My friends and I enjoyed the applause we received daily. It boosted our confidence and presence, knowing we performed on the same stage as many accomplished musicians and famous bands. The ragtime band members spent lots of time hanging out at the event before and after our sessions. This established and solidified many relationships for years to come. Both Jackie and Jerome frequently visited me at my home at Queen Street, since I lived so close to the conference center.

Jackie and I hung out most of the time. Some of the time, we joined the rest of the group. The two of us were so similar; we had to be different from everyone else. Our creativity and zest for adventure, our inquisitiveness and playfulness provoked us to develop our own code language over the years. No one understood the mystery of our language. Jackie's code name was Three-Seven and mine was Four-Five. That's how we always referred to each other. No one was let in on our secret code, well until now.

"Hey, Three-Seven! I've got a lecture now. Let's meet at four one five on the East Wing." Four-Five called out as I started walking in the direction of the lecture theater, with Three-Seven responding, "Four-Five, we need to make it at three five nine on the River End instead, then we can walk over to Paradise Island."

Anyone listening in on our conversation didn't have a clue as to what was being spoken. Places and people were all renamed. Classes were renamed.

Certain words were replaced by coined words that sounded like gibberish. Even our hello and goodbye greetings were coined.

Jerome visited me more than Jackie did. We usually hung out by the piano or sat in the living room chatting about music.

"Hey Chloe, do you know your piano stool is falling apart?" Jerome asked.

"Yeah, I know. I'll get my dad to fix it one of these days." I responded. Jerome picked up the stool, turned it around, and examined the fault.

"You know what, I'll fix it for you. I'll take it home with me today and bring it back in a few days. Can you manage without this stool until then?"

"Are you sure? You don't have to. And you want to carry the stool on the bus, take it to your home, fix it, and carry it back on the bus, then walk with it to my home again?"

"Yes, I'll do it. It's easy to fix." And so, Jerome carried my piano stool and took it home with him to fix it.

We were best friends. Chloe and Jerome. Chloe and Jackie. We spoke for hours on any subject. We shared secrets. We talked about life; the good and the bad. We made music together. Our friendships were built to last forever.

And then I remembered what Counselor had said to me when I was age nine,

"Not everyone is bad. There are many good people in the world. You'll find them on your journey of life. You have lots of friends who are waiting to meet you."

Counselor was right. Almost fourteen years later, I met two wonderful friends on the journey of my life. I had a sudden urge to meet with Counselor. The longing to see him and share everything.

Lying on my bed, with my eyes closed, in the safety of the darkness, I took a deep breath and exhaled. The familiar warmth washed over me as Counselor appeared. It was the same room colored in a myriad of white hues I had last seen him in the hospital corridor outside the theater. This time the both of us were sitting on chairs with an illusion of being hugged. I liked the comfort and tactility of hugging because I'm a big hugger. Settling in, caressing the fabric of the chair, and with a cheerful voice I said to him, "This feels so comfy."

"I'm glad you like it," he replied softly.

"Do you know what room this is?" he asked once he had my full attention.

"No," I said, "but I know this is where we spoke before I had my surgery."

"This is your Design Room," he offered, "And do you notice there are no pieces of anything here?" Scanning the room, I realized I couldn't see any seams.

"That's true. You're right. I hadn't noticed that." He continued.

"Everything is one continuous flow without any interruptions. In this room, all the pieces of your life are restored to your whole self. You'll begin to see your life as one long seamless journey. Here is where the pieces are sewn together to create an artwork with shades of white fluidity. Whites reflect off each other, and each unique piece reflects off each other as they come together in one glorious splash of waves."

I was stunned as he spoke.

"That's why you brought me here before my surgery," I spoke with an enlightened mind. "So my healing would be complete because you knew what would happen, right?"

"Yes, I did, Chloe. I did."

And with that, I fell into a sweet state of restful sleep.

CHAPTER 5
It's Happening Again

During the winter of 1985, the first Indian ragtime band had successfully made its debut in Durban. It was a notable historical moment not just for the Music Department at the University of Durban-Westville, but for thousands of Indian musicians who were not fortunate enough to make strides in their musical journey. After our initial stage nervousness, the band members slipped into the swing of things, sinking comfortably into the swell of the music. I savored the taste of freedom and fame. It didn't define me, but it definitely strengthened my confidence and crystallized my versatility as a reputable musician.

One evening, as the cool air moved invisibly among the gathering crowds beneath the vast expanse of starry skies, the band members played under the euphoric spell of music. Wings of romance fluttered in the air with couples holding hands, and whispering in each other's ears. The sounds of laughter and chatter in the crowds added human color to the intonation of clarinets and flutes. It seemed like the direction of the winds effortlessly and silently halted its course to a stillness. Happiness and joy hung like stars in the mesmerizing space of awe and beauty. Even the intangible things like time and sounds could be held and felt like an evocative pulse.

As I played the simple haunting melody of 'Stranger on the Shore,' I became distracted by the stranger among the crowds, watching me while we performed. I had never seen him before and wondered who he could be. He was quite a good-looking Indian guy, medium complexion, well dressed, an average frame and about five-feet-six-inches in height. I couldn't decipher why he was looking at me so intently.

At the end of our first set, I caught the stranger beckoning Jerome from the corner of my eye. They obviously knew each other, I thought as I leaned closer to Jackie, slightly turning away from him, "This guy talking to Jerome kept staring at me throughout the whole performance."

"I noticed. I wonder who he is. Hey, guess what? Looks like Jerome's bringing him over," Jackie said discreetly through her teeth. Instinctively, I wanted to turn and see for myself, but I resisted the urge.

"Chloe and Jackie, I'd like to introduce you to a friend of mine," Jerome smiled mischievously.

"This is George. George, this is Chloe, and this is Jackie." The message in Jerome's eyes was crystal clear since I knew him so well. George had apparently expressed an attraction for me. He smiled warmly as he stretched out his hand for a friendly handshake.

"Pleased to meet you. I really enjoyed the music," he spoke with a smoothly legato-like tone.

He sounded almost musical. George elaborated on the performance directing every word to me. Feeling uncomfortable and shy, not knowing where to look, I kept nodding my head in acknowledgment. If I looked at Jackie, I knew the both of us would burst out laughing, so I avoided her eyes.

As the conversation transitioned to an awkward exchange, Jerome and Jackie slowly exited the foursome leaving George and me alone.

Oh boy! I'm going to get those two for ditching me like this, I soundlessly murmured to myself as I fiddled with my hair nervously.

"I play the guitar for one of the jazz bands on the schedule," George said. "We're usually the last band on the schedule."

"Oh! That's nice!" not being able to think of anything else to say.

"So, how long have you been playing clarinet?" he asked to keep the conversation moving.

"Just over a year."

Over the next few minutes, he shared his passion for music, while I did most of the listening. I realized we had similar interests as he spoke. Looking at my watch, I said,

"It's almost time for the second set. I have to go."

"Is it okay if I wait for you after you've played? I really enjoyed talking to you."

"Sure." The truth was I still didn't know how to say no to people. But I did want to see him again I thought as I pensively played through the second set.

During the performance, George stood amongst the crowds and listened with his focus completely on me. I was unable to concentrate simply because I wasn't used to being the spotlight of someone's attention. Starting to feel a little nervous, I wasn't sure if this was how things worked with men and women. The only experience I had was with Jason at age fifteen.

After the set, George invited me to take a walk with him. I felt safe for two reasons: The place was packed with people, and he seemed kind and warm. Strolling along, the conversation became more natural, and I became more comfortable. He spoke about his job as a detective sharing examples of his adventures, while intentionally limiting the details to minimal facts. Without fail, he seamlessly navigated his way back to the subject of music. It was obvious! He loved playing the guitar.

George asked me questions about myself. He was captivated by everything I said, hanging on each word like dissolving candy floss. By the end of the evening, he gently brushed the back of my hand and playfully allowed his fingers to run over mine until we were holding hands. I was flustered and had no idea how to respond, but he continued to make me feel comfortable.

"Is it okay if I hold your hand?" he asked with a look of safety in his eyes.

I nodded without saying anything. I didn't know what to say. Now that we were holding hands, were we boyfriend and girlfriend? Was he supposed to say we were officially going out? I didn't know. I didn't have a clue. I was age twenty-three going onto age twenty-four, and I was utterly naïve and oblivious to red flags or green flags. I had never been on a date. No one had ever held my hand. No one had ever kissed me. No one was allowed to come closer, until now.

Maybe I knew that time was passing me by and the societal expectation of any girl at my age was marriage. Would George want to marry me? Would he make a good husband? Did I want to spend the rest of my life with him? Those questions went flying through my mind. I had no answers. The first day we met hadn't even ended, and I was thinking of marriage. Interrupting my own thoughts and whatever he was saying, I quickly said as I glanced at my watch,

"I have to get going. I have a curfew. My parents expect me to be home by 10:30 p.m."

"I could drop you off at home after my session if you like," he offered, anxiously waiting for me to agree. Panic buttons went off in my head,

"No, no, no. That's fine. I'm riding home with my friends."

"Okay, good. We can continue our conversation after your performance tomorrow." I nodded impatiently as he continued,

"I really enjoyed spending time with you, Chloe. I can't wait to see you tomorrow. Goodnight then."

"Goodnight," I said, lowering my eyes bashfully.

Walking away, I couldn't believe what had transpired over the last hour. My thoughts were in disarray. When I saw Jackie and Jerome, I didn't know what to say or how to describe what had happened as they eagerly looked at me waiting to hear the story. I was embarrassed. I could still feel the tingling where his rough masculine hands made contact with mine. I didn't know if it was a good thing or a bad thing.

That night when I got home, I was more confused about men. Who were they? Were they all alike? And where was Jason? He definitely wasn't coming back for me. He had probably forgotten me and moved on. There was no need to wait for him. Maybe this was my life partner. I had to ask Counselor for his advice. He would know what to say.

I showered as quickly as I could, jumped into bed and closed my eyes, waiting for Counselor. Immediately I found myself in the Design Room, sinking into the cushiony hugger chair with continuous lines and unstructured designs. The both of us gracefully settled into its comfort. Closing my eyes, I took a deep breath, inhaling the peaceful serenity surrounding me. He waited and watched me unfold and unwind from the tangled expressions and convoluted thoughts clouding my mind. Slowly uncoiling from the formless shape of confusion and obscurity, I waited for clarity and simplicity of mind.

"Chloe," he called me out of my thoughts into his presence. A sigh of relief escaped my lips as I opened my eyes to soak in the truthfulness of his aura. Taking in my surroundings, I asked, "Why are we still here Counselor?" I knew there had to be a reason. Counselor was intentional about every detail. I just knew it. Without waiting for his response, I asked again.

"Why am I here again? Does this have to do with George?" He nodded his head in agreement and began to explain to me,

"When you're physically sick and your body needs healing, your system is built to restore itself. You can heal if you're willing to rest and follow the doctor's orders." He waited a moment before he went on,

"But when your heart opens itself to relationships, there are risks. Those risks involve both good and bad experiences. The heart isn't built to restore itself if it breaks. It needs help. The only way I can help you is when you help yourself. You'll have to learn to love yourself first before you open your heart to anyone. Chloe, you're a loving soul, and you love freely. In your friendships, you give your everything without expecting anything in return. When you get hurt, it's very difficult for the pieces to reflect off each other. The heart thinks and reacts differently than the body. If you love yourself first, you'll never allow anyone to treat you anyhow. So, when your heart breaks, this is the place you come back to, your Design Room. This is where you can restore and renew so you can feel whole again."

"Where does George fit into all of this?" As if reading my mind, he went on,

"Remember in the Design Room, all the pieces come together as one continuous flow, like one continuous journey. Your life is a series of pieces that all fit together. You may not be able to see the whole picture, but as you continue to grow and experience life, you'll begin to see glimpses of who you are. Only then you will begin to understand your life's purpose, little by little. In this room, the clutter and confusion will give way to clarity and direction."

I understood. Without Counselor answering any of the questions that plagued my mind, I was catching a glimpse of the bigger picture.

"I get it, Counselor. I finally get it." I said with enlightenment.

"I know you do, Chloe. You have been given the gift of wisdom, which means you're able to see and understand the human heart and mind in a deeper way than many other people. It's easy to see things objectively with others, and still be empathetic and non-judgmental. But when it comes to matters of your heart, your emotions will cloud your judgment. That's why you have to always be on the alert, carefully assessing which ones are red flags and which ones are green flags. Always remember that a plan may work perfectly in your mind, but doesn't translate the same way in life because the world isn't perfect. Many things are outside of your control including people. The only thing in your control is You."

It was a lot for me to absorb, yet I was captivated by every word and soaked in Counselor's wisdom. I could sit and listen to him talk forever, and still be completely fascinated. He knew all the answers. He always knew what to say. He answered questions I didn't know to ask. With renewed conviction, I repeated the words of a nine-year-old girl, "One day I'm going to be a counselor just like you."

With that, I slipped into a peaceful night's rest. Tomorrow is another day, and I was ready to take on the challenge, not realizing it was easier said than done.

The next day when I awoke, my stomach was in knots. I was anxious about the performances. No, I was anxious about seeing George again. Was this supposed to be love? It somehow lacked the safety I had felt with Jason, but I remembered that Jason was gone. He was not coming back. This was my life now. Reflecting and putting some perspective to it, by no means eliminated the overtaking anxiety. By the time I arrived at the event, my nerves were tightly wound. He was already there, waiting for me. As soon as he saw me, he walked over smiling,

"Hello, Chloe."

"Hello, George."

"I haven't stopped thinking about you. I couldn't wait to see you today. I hope you don't mind that I got here earlier than you expected." Forcing a tiny smile, I said,

"No, that's okay," even though I wasn't completely okay with it.

Somehow, he had a way of making me feel comfortable. Maybe it was his tone or the tender breathiness of his voice. I couldn't pinpoint what it was, even though I had a really keen ear as a musician. My musicality didn't help me at all. The conversation continued as the band members assembled their instruments. The first set seemed to go quicker than usual, although I wished it took a little longer. Between sets, we talked. After the second set, we talked, strolling through the event park among the crowds.

As the days passed, this became the routine, and I grew more comfortable. By the fifth day, he casually bent over and brushed his lips against mine. My heart raced. I didn't know if I was nervous or afraid. Maybe both. It was the first time I had been kissed, and I liked it. The next day, I waited for him to kiss me again, and he did. By the end of the week, the kiss deepened into something foreign. I didn't know if I liked it or disliked it. When I got home that night, with urgency, I brushed my teeth and my tongue as hard as I could. A sense of violation and fear had crept in. I'd seen other couples kissing the same way. Maybe this is how it was supposed to be. If that were the case, then I would have to get used to it. Bracing myself, I decided I would give it another try.

When George kissed me the next day, I was ready to explore the unknown with him, after all, he was now my boyfriend. Every day got better and better. I was adjusting to this new exploration and discovered something new every moment.

Expo 85 was an unforgettable experience etched on the walls of my mind. As the season drew to a close, I wondered what would happen between us. Without realizing it, he had grown on me. The door of my heart had been left ajar, and George slid through the crack. At night, I thought about him and replayed our interactions with beautiful details. Counselor wasn't on my mind. George was. He was my last thought at night and first thought in the morning. He was the true prince, who was sent to save the princess from herself.

The time had arrived for me to say something to my parents. George wanted to keep seeing me. He told me that he loved me; wanted to marry me. It was like a fairytale and just when I thought princes didn't exist in real life.

One evening when I got home, I went straight to my parents and told them about George. "Dad, Mom, I met someone at Expo 85. He's a nice Christian guy, and he likes me."

"Do you know him well?" my father asked. "Who introduced him to you?" Together, they fired a barrel of questions at me.

"He's a friend of Jerome's. He's a real gentleman. I spoke to him a few times at the event," I replied, choosing my words very carefully.

"But is he serious about you? Does he want to marry you?"

"He told me he wants to marry me and he wants to meet you," I confirmed.

My parents, agreeing to my request, still had reservations. They wanted to meet him before allowing a stranger to court their daughter. The next day after the show, I asked Jerome to come along with George to the flat. My parents trusted Jerome. When dad and mom met George, they liked him immediately because he was very amicable and personable. And so, when Expo 85 ended, George came by every day after work. We had dinner together, spent time in the living room with the rest of the family, and played music together.

"Here," I said, "George, come and listen to this."

I proceeded to play 'Misty' on the piano using simple chords. When I finished playing the piece, he said to me, "Why don't you try this?" and introduced me to the magical world of jazz.

He showed me how to substitute a simple major chord with a major seventh chord adding color and sophistication to the tune. I was excited about this new approach to music and was delighted that my boyfriend had taught it to me.

George had been visiting for a couple of months. I enjoyed having him around. He was considerate and affectionate, and we explored music together. I couldn't believe how lucky I was. This was every girl's dream, and I was living it. It was a warm summer evening. As usual, I walked George to the front door to say goodnight. We lingered outside like we did every night sneaking a quick kiss when no one was looking. As I pulled away from him, I noticed a red mark on his neck. My heart went cold.

"Who gave you a love bite?" I was afraid to hear his response. He looked guilty but shrugged it off with ease as he answered,

"You did. Don't you remember?"

I was confused. "No, I didn't. I don't remember ever giving you a love bite."

My head was spinning. I began to doubt myself. Did I kiss his neck and didn't realize it? I don't know how to give love bites, so maybe I did. He was looking at me observing how confused I seemed. With a reassuring tone he said, "Remember when you kissed me the other day? We were standing right here."

How come I don't remember, I thought to myself, not fully convinced.

"But I don't remember." I wasn't sure if I believed him or believed myself. Something didn't feel right. My thoughts were in a tizzy. *George won't lie. He loves me. He spends every evening with me, and he calls me from work every day to say he loves me.*

I tried desperately to convince myself, pushing aside my jumbled thoughts. He naturally took me into the security of his arms, told me how much he loved me, kissed me goodnight, and left. It was already past 10 p.m.

A few days later, Jerome visited. There was a concerned look in his eyes. I knew something was wrong, and tried to figure out what was so important. As soon as we were alone in the living room, he said, "When I went to visit George, his mother was there. He wasn't home. She said he will never marry you because she already chose a wife for him. The girl practically lives in his house. So, Chloe you better stop seeing him. He's not going to marry you. He'll never disappoint his mother even if he loves you."

I refused to believe it was true. I didn't want to accept it. I told Jerome that George will never leave me because he loves me.

"Chloe," Jerome warned, "I don't want you to get hurt, and he's going to hurt you."

"No, he won't," I almost cried. "He'll never hurt me."

Jerome didn't bring it up again. He couldn't stand to see me in this state. A few weeks passed, nothing was said, and the subject wasn't brought up by either George, Jerome or myself. The matter was put to rest.

In the meantime, my uncle had planned a family dinner party at his house. George was invited to go along. The phone rang, and it was George.

"I'm running late at work. I should be there in half hour." When my mother heard that he was going to be late, she said with impatience,

"Jacob, let's go. We can't make these people wait for us. Chloe can stay home and wait for George. He can bring her to the dinner." My dad agreed it was a good idea. Everyone left to my uncle's house while I waited for George.

There was knock on the door. Immediately I recognized it. I had grown accustomed to his sound. Happily, I opened the door with a smile on my face. He looked at me strangely, and I didn't think anything of it. I thought he was upset because he had to work late. Holding my gaze, he walked in slowly, closed the door and locked it behind him with ease. Uncertain about his mood I asked,

"George, is everything okay? Why are you locking the door? We have to go. Everyone is waiting for us." He leered at me as he approached.

I still had no idea what was up with him. He kissed me, and I thought that could be it. Maybe it was because we were alone for the first time at home. We had privacy. Neither of us had to worry about anyone barging in. That had to be it. He gently guided me towards the wall deepening the kiss into something more intense than usual. It frightened me, and I tried to push him away. He ignored my movements and continued to lean heavily on me. For the first time in my life, I felt a man's arousal pressing against me. Thoughts of Jimmy came flooding back as I tried to push them away,

This is not Jimmy. This is not Jimmy. George is not Jimmy.

Trapped! There was no place for me to run, nowhere I could hide, no one I could call. Nothing. Caught between him and the wall, I instinctively knew what was about to happen. My dreams shattered into pieces. Shock tore apart the strength I had so carefully stored up inside myself. I had let my guard down. I had left the door of my heart opened. I had ignored the red flags. It was happening all over again.

As I felt him, my heart banged furiously against my ribcage. I couldn't think. I couldn't make sense of what was going on. I tried to push him away as I feebly repeated the most difficult word in my world,

"No! No! No!"

George wasn't listening. He grabbed me and pushed me towards the bedroom. How could this be the same wonderful man who treated me so kindly for the past few months? How was that possible? Who was the man in front of me? What had happened to George? What did he do to George?

He unbuttoned my blouse, roughly pulled it off before pushing me onto the bed. Without any warning, he dropped his pants and was on top of me. It was all happening so fast. Flashes of a nine-year-old girl came flooding into my conscious mind. I tried to look into his eyes and say, "Please don't," but they were blank and cold. I tried my best to hold back my screams of pain; in my heart and between my legs. My mind was racing like it needed to get to the finish line.

Chloe is a good girl. Chloe is a good girl. Chloe is a good girl, was all I could say to myself.

It seemed to go on endlessly. This stranger on top of me had no idea who I was. He didn't even know my name. He couldn't have known my name because not once did he say my name.

Chloe, it will be over soon, I tried to comfort myself.

After he was done, he declared with authority, "Now you belong to me, and no one will ever have you. You are mine."

He was blind to my tears. No words of love were spoken. He didn't even say he loved me. He seemed angry. He stood, pulling his pants up and said in a flat, emotionless voice, "Get ready. We need to leave. I don't want anyone wondering why we're taking so long."

Slowly I sat up, picked up my clothes and covered myself as I made my way to the bathroom.

Chloe is a good girl, I insisted. But I knew one thing was for sure-I would never trust a man again. I would live with a closed heart and wait for the day I die. There was nothing else left.

I withdrew into myself. George continued visiting, pretending as though nothing had happened. The sentences in our conversations had drastically shortened to phrases.

A week later, my father received a call from a woman who said she was George's aunt. After explaining how she was related, the sister of George's mother, she went on to say,

"George's mother asked me to call you and let you know she has already chosen a wife for George. The girl is at his house every day, and on weekends she stays over."

"But George spends every evening with Chloe, so how can he be spending time with this girl?"

"When he gets home every night, he has to drop her off at her house," she said. "And over the weekends she sleeps in his room."

My dad couldn't believe what he was hearing. As soon as he put the phone down, he called me into the living room and related the conversation. I acted as if I couldn't believe it and yet deep down there was a nagging, persistent feeling. When George arrived after work, my dad immediately addressed it. The color drained from his face. Dad and I knew it was the truth.

"My mother wants me to marry her, and she invites her to the house," George tried to explain.

"When I get home, I'm forced to drop her off at her house. I don't love her. I love Chloe, and I want to marry Chloe," he spoke with deep sadness.

"As long as she comes over to your house and she stays over the weekend, you can't see Chloe," my father said firmly.

"You are not allowed to come back here until you sort things out with your mother and this girl."

"But my mother won't listen to me. I won't be able to stop this girl from visiting my home. My mother keeps inviting her over."

"Then you can't come back here, and you have to forget about Chloe."

With that, George walked out of the flat and didn't come back. History was repeating itself. Feeling beaten down, I had an idea.

What if we eloped, then George would be forced to marry me. After all we had slept together. That was my belief! If two people eloped, that would mean they had sex, then society would expect them to get married. I had no idea the world didn't work like that. The more I thought about my idea, the more determined I was. I just had to convince George it was our only option.

The next morning, my mind was made up. I packed a duffel bag, and let it down through the bedroom window, landing on the corridor floor. Walking hastily to the front door, I called out to my mother, "I'm off to university. See you later," hurriedly, I quickened my steps, grabbed my bag and ran down ten flights of stairs until I got to the ground floor.

Instead of making my way to university, I headed to my friend's place about twenty minutes away. After explaining everything to Fran, I asked her if I could spend the night until I figured something out. Fran agreed. I called George and asked him to come over. Within a few minutes, I heard the old familiar knock on the door and the same distant look in his eyes. He kissed me as usual, then listened to me relate the events of the day.

"George, I did something daring today."

"What did you do?" He asked as though I had done something wrong. I sensed it in his tone.

"I ran away from home. I thought if we elope then we can be together. Our families will be forced to get us married."

"I will never disappoint my mother."

"But you said you love me and you want to marry me?" I cried.

He didn't respond. Not a word. Not a sound. Not a sigh. He just looked at me and didn't commit to anything. Suddenly like a light switch, the truth spoke in silence.

There was no prince to save Chloe. It was over.

The next day, I returned home. My dad and mom were happy to have me back, safe and sound. Instead of being angry with me, they were loving and kind. There was no mention of George ever again. They didn't ask me what had transpired and I didn't say anything. It was a closed story. But my heart was bleeding.

CHAPTER 6
The Magical World of Jazz

As I lay my weary head on my pillow, oblivious to its softness and comfort, my cold heart beat like a distant hollow drum. I was like the sleeping dead, austere yet restless.

"You will live again, Chloe," the old familiar voice injected life into my veins.

I knew I was back in the garden of my heart. For a few moments, I allowed the infusion to repair my broken soul, piece by piece. I submerged myself in the living sounds of water rushing over my soul, as I conceded to the gravitational force stronger than me. Taking the form of its original shape, my soul succumbed to the cultivator of the garden.

Slowly opening my eyelids to behold the surroundings, I found myself laying on a bed of rose petals. Someone had removed the thorns. I felt the pain in my memory, but the silkiness of the roses caressed the cracks of my soul. Inhaling the sweetness of its scent mixed with the stench of pain, I tried desperately to separate the two. Lingering somewhere in the midst of the roses, I reminded myself I was human. I remembered Counselor's words,

"The heart isn't built to restore itself. It needs help. The only way I can help you is when you help yourself."

I knew I had to find a way to help myself. Being here with Counselor was the only way I knew how. Somehow, I had to make my way to the Design Room within my heart. Forcing myself, I pushed against my elbows, until I picked myself up and stood in the middle of the rose garden. The floor of the soil was covered with a thick carpet of petals, a lush pile causing my feet to sink into its pleasure. Looking around, I gasped at the sight of the beautiful garden. It was mine. I took a graceful step, pressing on the petals as it released oils of rose delights, massaging the soles of my feet, traveling upwards until it reached my innermost thoughts, diffusing the hidden sorrow. I realized I had broken into a small smile.

Encompassed by the wonder of it all, I approached the natural bath in front of me, gurgling with utter delight. This was the living sound of water I heard. Stepping into it, I welcomed the trickling stream caressing my feet, soothing my weary soles as it carried the weight of my body without complaint. I lowered myself into the bath of enchanted healing waters until I was fully immersed and completely covered with rose petals. For a quick moment, I had forgotten the crooked cracks of my soul. I had forgotten the memories of pain. I was finding a way to heal myself. It would take time. It would be a process. I was human after all. But one day I will be whole again, I told myself. I didn't realize I was already in a healing process.

Emerging from the pools of healing waters, dripping with oils of solace and placidity, I looked around. Counselor was nowhere to be seen. Where could he be? He was always here. Confused, I tried to fathom why he was missing when suddenly I heard his voice in my heart,

"And when your heart breaks, this is the place you come back to, your Design Room. This is where you can restore and renew so you can feel whole again."

With excitement and anticipation, I quickened my pace as I made my way to the Big Red Heart in the middle of the garden. Placing my hand on the Big Red Heart, I closed my eyes and waited until I could hear the rhythm of my heartbeat. I then listened carefully to hear Counselor's heartbeat. They were not aligned. Anxiously, I waited for their synchronicity, but they still didn't align. Taking a deep breath, I felt a slowing down as I listened once more.

Sure enough, both heartbeats were steering their way to each other. A clicking sound unlocked the door of the Big Red Heart. The magnetic force of his presence was overpowering in my heart, drawing me closer to him. As I placed my hand on the Design Room door, it immediately swung open. He was there, waiting. I rushed into his embrace as the flood unleashed itself on his shirt. He held me, waiting until I subsided. I felt a lightness overtake me. I had been in a stupor of disbelief. Seeing Counselor brought me back to the reality of what had transpired in my life.

"I came to see how the pieces fit together," I cried. "I know everything happens for a reason. I want to know the reason."

"Everything that happens doesn't always happen for a reason, but you can find a reason in it. Some things may not make sense, but all things have a place in your purpose, and this is where you find your purpose. The Healing Baths will heal the unseen wounds of your heart like a salve. It's a time of reflection and contemplation. The cracks in your heart will fade, but never disappear. However, it will bring new meaning to your life. You'll find purpose hidden in every crack and every scar. Right now, it's hard to see, but if you keep coming back, you'll begin to see the larger picture. The brokenness of your heart, will one day reveal itself, as the hidden treasure. It will become your fiery strength."

So, what I had experienced, was the Healing Baths! I believed every word Counselor said. Although I couldn't fully understand the wisdom within, I saw glimpses of the future. A spark was all I needed, to hope!

There were two universities in Durban; one for whites and the other for non-whites. The University of Natal had majority of white students. A handful of Indian students made the cut due to their exceptional talent. When I was in my final year, a Jazz Department was launched for the first time in South African history. Curious about its offerings, I made queries about the program. To be considered, I had to audition with Darius Brubeck. That meant playing a jazz piece on the piano. I certainly didn't know any sophisticated jazz chords or how to improvise. The only piece I knew was 'Misty.' George had taught me a few major seventh and minor seventh chords. That must have been good enough because I was accepted into the program. I had to repeat my third year to specialize in Jazz Studies. To graduate, I had to complete at least two years of the Jazz core curriculum. Being accepted into the program was an honor, especially since I didn't know how to play jazz piano. Obviously, Darius thought I had something in my style. Having a keen musician's ear was in my favor. I decided to go for it since I'd already lost a whole year during the time of my surgery. *What was one more year, if I spent it doing something that fascinated me?*

It was one of the best decisions I had made in my life.

Being the only Indian female jazz pianist in the Jazz Department was both exhilarating and thrilling. As long as I can remember, I always craved the unusual, the outstanding, and the exceptional. Being different was a thrill for me. It somehow gave me a high. Studying under the direction of Darius Brubeck was an unforgettable experience. He introduced me to the magical world of jazz. His patience and constant encouragement motivated me to keep trying, even when I felt like my improvisations sucked. Learning new chord structures and extensions opened my mind to the sounds I had never heard before. I learned to play the blues and jazz standards. I learned bebop and progressive jazz. Everything was fascinating and exploratory.

Within six months, I had developed basic jazz skills to join the Jazz Ensemble. At the first band practice session, I sat nervously at the piano, wondering if I'd be able to take the solo when the time came. Darius counted the band in, and the music began.

After a few solos, Darius turned and looked at me to cue me in. Far from relaxed, with tense muscles that inhibited my flexibility, I played my first solo to George Gershwin's 'I Got Rhythm.' Fingers slipping awkwardly across the keys, improvising over the chord changes, I made it through thirty-two bars of music. When I was done, I looked up at Darius, as he smiled at me in acknowledgment. I could tell he was pleased with my improvisation. I did it. I took my first jazz solo in a band. It may not have been virtuosic, but it was a solo. That was a fantastic achievement for me! How I wished I had done four whole years in Jazz! The two years I spent learning the beautiful art of improvisation, was life-changing for me.

Right around the same time, my family joined one of the largest multi-racial churches in the city. It was the first church in Durban that opened their doors to all races. Whites, Indians, Coloreds, and Blacks flocked to the church, hungry to know what life was like outside their closed world. International guest speakers came from everywhere, fascinated by the multicultural congregation and the heavenly harmonies produced by the African voices. It was unlike any sound they'd heard before. On the other hand, South African musicians were mesmerized by the music produced in the United States. We tried to mimic American customs, songs and musical arrangements. Listening to an American accent was like melting butter, smooth and creamy. As far as South Africans were concerned, anyone with an American accent was immediately categorized as a superior race, irrespective of color.

I was fortunate to be exposed and actively involved with different race groups, both at the university and at the church. My friends were from all four race groups, and I was beginning to understand the cultural dynamics, and learned how to have cultural dexterity at a time when the country was volatile. My sister, Charlee, and I made lots of friends at the Young Adults meeting.

Charlee's friend, Sean, who was white, invited us to his flat for dinner. When we got to the building, she couldn't remember his flat number. We buzzed the manager of the building on the intercom, thinking he would be able to provide the correct flat number. His strong Afrikaans accent came through the intercom. "Wait right there! I'm coming downstairs."

Relieved that the manager was going to direct us to Sean's place, we waited for him, not suspecting a thing. The glass security doors were forcefully flung open, and out came a vicious looking white male in his fifties, charging at us with a gun pointing in our direction. "Get out, you coolie!" he screamed, "Get out now before I have you arrested."

Understanding the color of my skin was setting him off, I tried to explain in a submissive tone that we were invited. It made him angrier. "Sean is expecting us for dinner. Please call him and check with him."

The manager refused to hear what we had to say. He brought the barrel of his gun close to my forehead and began swearing and using foul language, as his face turned red with anger. He looked dangerous. I was now convinced he would pull the trigger if I said another word. "Get out! You brown coolie! Get out! Get out!" Frightened by his outrage, I looked at Charlee and quietly said, "Come, let's go!" We walked out, with him screaming and swearing as we exited the building.

That was a big lesson for us. We faced racism in its coldest ugliest cruelest form, and I knew I would never see things in the same way again. It was my defining moment. I was non-white, and the color of my skin determined my future. I decided on that day I would stand for my race, my color, my gender, my talent; it is who I am and who God created me to be. I am not a mistake. I do not have the wrong color. I am as I was intended to be. Chloe.

Within a few months of joining the church, I was invited to play in the praise band as the keyboard player. Of course, my exceptional skills opened doors of opportunity all over the city. Feeling humiliated, since the keyboard felt like a step down from the piano, I submitted to the white authority in the church. It was the only way I could move ahead in my music.

Faithfully, I attended practice sessions and played at multiple Sunday services. Other pianists were always asking me to teach them jazz chords and licks, which I willingly did. If I was not playing keyboard, then I played the Hammond organ. I could rattle the organ in true gospel style. People loved the swell of the music filling the auditorium. Some of the visiting international speakers grew accustomed to my sound. When I wasn't on stage, they would specifically ask for me. I became well-known as the Indian girl who sounded jazzy on the piano and the organ at the largest non-denomination church in the city.

As thousands of people gathered every Sunday, I allowed myself to adjust to the crowds, easing into a comfort zone. I didn't like the fact that most of the leadership in this multiracial non-denominational church were Whites, but what could I do. That was the life of a non-white South African! Because of the color of my skin, I didn't hold any leadership position even though I had the highest form of education in the band.

Well, that was until things unexpectedly changed overnight! A famous gospel singer from America, Alvin Slaughter, visiting South Africa, was scheduled to perform at the church for two nights. No one knew what tracks he would be singing. None of the musicians on stage knew what to expect. I sat at the grand piano, waiting in anticipation for the first note to be sung.

Again, what I did have in my favor was a very musical ear. Anything I heard, I could immediately produce it on the piano without even practicing it.

The singer sang the first few notes of the song. I listened. My fingers fumbled on the keys for a quick second until I slipped into the same note he sang with ease. My left hand joined the right hand, accompanying him as though we had thoroughly rehearsed the song. In the middle of the performance, the artist couldn't resist turning around and saying to me,

"If you keep playing that way Chloe, I'll have to take you with me to America."

After that public acknowledgment in front of thousands of people, a meeting was called up. On the second day, before the service, I was officially given the title of Music Director. What a momentous occasion! An Indian woman in a leadership position! A turning point for me and for the history of the church. A new chapter had begun! I gained confidence and developed my stage presence over the next few months. Instead of stage fright, I felt energized whenever I was on stage. For the first time in my life, I found my identity. My own special brand! Soon, I began to expand my musical skills through musical arrangements for the band and the choir. Music filled my life, and I forgot all about the cracks and the scars under the surface of my emerging identity.

Counselor knew this was what I needed. He gave me the space to explore my creativity with limitless possibilities. Although music governed my life, I continued my conversations with Counselor, but not as long as before. The gift of music I possessed was healing me without me realizing it. I knew the cracks were still there, but the pain had diminished into a faraway ache that transformed into melodies and musical sounds.

There were four students in the Jazz Studies program graduating in the same year. Two of us were completing our undergraduate degree. As part of our final practical exams, we had to do a full-length concert, showcasing our skills. The acoustics in the hall carried the voices of people chatting and browsing through the program pages before the start of the concert. My hands suddenly turned cold and sweaty. Oh boy, was I nervous! All four of us played different instruments, so we formed a perfect quartet; saxophone, piano, bass, and drums. Seated in the audience were our three examiners. We were ready to go.

The first set featured all four of us. We opened with 'Airegin,' a bebop jazz standard by Sonny Rollins. After each solo, the audience clapped. I couldn't wait for my improvisation to come to an end because I still wasn't comfortable playing bebop. The audience applauded after my solo, even though it was nothing fantastic. I think they applauded because an Indian female jazz pianist was on stage. An unusual sighting! It was a first for everyone! People were excited, especially all my friends and family, who kept cheering me on. The rest of the set went smoothly, as jazz music filled the auditorium. My thoughts kept rushing to the second half, and I had to keep pulling it back to the moment. There was a reason for that. My main solo piano performance for the night was the kick-off for the second set.

During the interval, I tried my best to relax. We were allowed to mingle with the guests in the lobby area. My chest started to tighten, my fingers were icy, my palms were sweaty, and I felt stiffness, rather than flexibility in my fingers.

"This is going to be bad," I said to myself. "This is going to be good," I heard a voice coming from the stage.

Curiously I made my way to the front of the hall, but no one was there. Just the Steinway grand piano waiting for me to bring it to life. Again, I heard, "This is going to be good."

Following the sound of the voice backstage, I couldn't see anyone. At least this gave me a moment away from the crowds to pull myself together. I closed my eyes and exhaled deeply as I released the tension I had built up. I guess it was performance nerves.

Suddenly, I saw him smiling at me. Caught up in my anxiety, I had almost forgotten Counselor. He took my icy hands in his and rubbed them against his warm, worn hands. My muscles began to relax. My hands warmed up. My head felt lighter. My chest felt free. The spirit of a true artist emerged from within. An aching to touch the keys and play to my heart's content, overtook me. The audience must have been seated for a few minutes because I heard my name, followed by a resounding applause. It was time!

I walked over to the piano like I was walking on air. I felt lost in the musical notes I could hear in my head, eagerly waiting to make its way to my fingers. I sat on the piano stool, adjusted its distance and placed my hands on the keys. Closing my eyes for a moment, I heard this affirmation, *Chloe will draw people into her music to an experiential place.* There was silence in the room. The music in my heart felt like it bypassed my head, and traveled through my fingers to the keys intuitively. My fingers were in total obedience to the music inside of me. *Sounds of Lament* by J.J Johnson replaced the silence. It filled the space and resonated in a continuous ebb and flow, until it climaxed, taking all those under its spell, deeper and higher into the state of unexplained beauty. After reaching a crescendo, the music began its descent with pleasing ease, resolving itself on its final note. An intense flicker of silence was broken by the standing applause that seemed to go on forever. I will never forget that moment. Nothing could stop me now. Nothing! I believed nothing was impossible if I just tried. Nothing!

A few weeks later, my results arrived. I did it! I finally graduated with my Bachelor's Degree, two years later than anticipated. It didn't feel believable, but it was. Plus, my specialization in Jazz Studies had only taken me two years, instead of four. I was over the moon! Immediately, I enrolled in the Master's program in Jazz Composition and Orchestration and received a full scholarship. There were only two Graduate Assistant positions available every year, and it was given to the two top students. I was one of them. I held this position for four years.

My skills as a performer continued to develop, as I learned the art of arranging and composing for orchestra and big bands. The exposure to these new sounds started to grow on me. Listening to arrangements and deconstructing them taught me the fine skills of orchestration. The music in my head was swelling. At that time, no one used software programs like Finale. We had to notate every note with a pencil from the conductor's score to the individual instruments. Night after night, I made little round heads with attached stems. It was an endless task. I couldn't get the notes fast enough from my head onto the staff. Pages and pages of musical notes sprawled across the lines. But I loved it.

There was also another element to composing and arranging. I had to write a dissertation of one hundred pages on a musical piece or some controversial topic where I could prove my argument. After researching for hours in the library, since it wasn't in the day of Google, I stumbled upon something that caught my interest. 'Porgy and Bess' was the first black opera written by George and Ira Gershwin. All the reviews at the time of production dismissed it as an opera. That got me thinking. Then why did George Gershwin say it was an opera? There had to be facts to substantiate it. And why did the critics dispute it? On what grounds? And so, the search began.

Completing my postgrad took me another four years. Later in my story, I'll expand on this and share some of the interesting facts I discovered and the people I met. It was pretty fascinating! While working on my postgrad studies, I continued to develop my musical skills as an arranger in the church I was attending. With the knowledge, I had gained, and a place to immediately apply some of the techniques I learned, my level of expertise began to gain momentum.

One Sunday stands out for me. Many wonderful things were happening amidst all the not-so-wonderful things. I had Counselor. I had my music. I had Ama. I had many great friends. Things just can't get any better than that, right? And I know that Counselor was the master orchestrator in bringing all of this together, as though he had composed the symphony of my life. He did it by counseling me through our deep conversations over the years.

My perspective kept growing and changing from one level to the next. Sometimes, the past would creep up on me, but I didn't stay there, I went to the Big Red Heart to get me back on track. I don't think the past ever goes away, but the kind of power it had over me did change. It became my fiery strength and the desire to pursue what most people thought was unattainable.

That Sunday morning, I was scheduled to play the piano in church. I knew in advance there was a guest speaker. He belonged to the church prior to me joining and had immigrated to the USA. He was a well-known, accomplished pianist with a fine jazz feel to his music and a rare gift of prophecy. I had heard him once before. A few family members and friends had gone to one of his meetings. During the service, he publicly mentioned a few identifying features pointing to me. There was no way I was going to stand up and reveal myself. Friends sitting next to me leaned over and whispered, "Chloe, he's referring to you." I shook my head in disagreement. To my amazement, in a crowd of over fifteen hundred people, he asked me, "Is that you?"

Shocked and self-conscious, I nodded my head. He called me forward and said, "Many waves of change will sweep over people. Your music will bring a new sound of healing, restoration, and hope in every transition." I didn't fully grasp the meaning of it all, but stored the words in my heart.

Now that I belonged to the church, I was excited about his visit. He was in town for a few performances. People in the city of Durban were in anticipation and from the looks of it, every performance was going to be a full house.

There he sat in the front row as I played, and he didn't take his eyes off me. He knew the other piano players well. I was a new face. It could have been pride, but I wanted him to hear me play. No one else had a jazz touch to their piano playing like I did. It somehow felt like kindred spirits.

After the regular worship singing, he came on stage and took his place at the piano. It was breathtaking. As he began to play, something evoked in the atmosphere. He played with an otherworldly sound, like sounds from some heavenly celestial place. We were captivated by the divine presence that seemed to take up every space in the theater. Thousands of people were present. I had never seen or experienced anything like it before. I knew we had a connection. I just didn't know what or how. He was affectionately referred to as Prophet Zach.

Songs I had never heard before left his lips as he sang. He spoke, and then he sang again. Words he was saying were accurate and futuristic. He called people by their names without knowing who they were. He told them their life stories. I was baffled. How did he know such things? Something was different about him, something mysterious and unusual. I just had to find a way to get to talk to him. At the end of the meeting, he called the music team together and said, "I have a few performances, and I need musicians. I'd like to practice with all of you on Thursday evening. Does that work for everyone?"

I didn't even give it a second thought before I said, "That works for me." He looked over at me, and said,

"I have cassettes of the songs I'd like to sing. Can you work out the arrangements for them?" Was this really happening? Was he asking me to work on his arrangements? I gently nodded my head. The words didn't make it out of my mouth. This felt like another dream. What an excellent opportunity to work with Prophet Zach! With that, he said,

"See you all on Thursday evening."

That was the beginning of a new chapter in my life. I didn't want to awaken from all my beautiful dreams. My life was amazing. I was so happy.

I spent the next few days working out the arrangements to the songs. I finally knew why I was studying Jazz Composing and Arranging at the University. It was preparing me for this very thing. Although I struggled with some of the parts, I just kept trying,

Chloe can do this. Chloe's got what it takes.

When it got to Thursday, I was full of excitement because I had figured out the arrangements. I sketched out the musical format of the songs with the chords and the arrangement entry points. I couldn't really notate them on staff because most of the musicians couldn't read music.

Thursday was the beginning of a beautiful relationship between a mentor and his mentee. Yes, Prophet Zach became my mentor for many years. He taught me how to listen to the sounds of heaven, while sitting at the piano. He taught me how to sing a new song every time I'm on stage without having sung it before. He taught me how to play the piano evocatively by using my improvisatory skills in a new way. He taught me how to tap into the spirit of each man, then play and sing a song that spoke to the inner core of who they were.

The performances were captivating! No one wanted to leave the theater at the end of the performances. I loved playing on stage with him. We were all caught up in the meditative bubble of his musical creations. It carried us to places deep inside of ourselves with peace and serenity, to places outside of ourselves in a world of limitless possibilities.

The next few weeks were complete bliss. The art I learned on stage, didn't only happen on stage. When I got home, I practiced this unique art on my piano for hours. I realized Prophet Zach must have done the same thing. The more I played and sang new songs, the more fluent I became, the more comfortable I became with the spirit world. There was no turning back for me. I had to talk to Counselor about everything that was going on. He would enlighten me. He always did. Counselor always knew the answers to the most challenging questions.

I must have played for about two hours non-stop before I headed to bed. There was no way I was going to fall off to sleep. I was too wired. Closing my eyes, I found myself in the Dark Room. I couldn't see anything.

"Open your eyes, Chloe," came that familiar voice.

"Does it matter if I open my eyes or keep them closed?" I asked.

"You do want to see, don't you?" I felt he was going somewhere with this. Every word counts with Counselor. There are no unintentional words.

"Yes, I do," I gave in to the mystery he was about to unfold.

"What do you see?" he asked.

"It's dark. I can't see a thing," I spoke the truth.

"Look again, Chloe!" he asked for the second time. "What do you see?"

I didn't know what to look for or how to look. I tried hard to see something, but there was nothing. Maybe this wasn't going to work for me. Perhaps this is a gift only for Prophet Zach. Perhaps he was the only one who could see. I started to give up when I heard a phrase from the lyrics of one of the songs, 'Piercing the darkness.' What does that mean? I sang it without knowing what it meant. How do I pierce the darkness? Then it suddenly dawned on me. The only thing that has the power to penetrate the darkness is light.

"Chloe, if you look in the darkness for answers, you won't find it. But if you look for the light, then the darkness will slowly disappear, and the answers will be revealed."

"How did I miss that? It's so simple, but why didn't I see that before? It's not complicated at all to understand."

"Chloe, every secret thing is simple. Every wise word is simple. If you look for answers in complexities, you won't find it. If you remain baffled, you won't be able to look for the light in the darkness. If you try too hard, you won't find the light." He kept giving me clues. Every clue brought me closer to the truth. What happened next was bewildering!

"I can see!" I shouted out in excitement.

At first, there were blurred images. My eyes were beginning to adjust to the darkness and soft light gently illuminated the room. I realized I had stopped focusing on the darkness while Counselor and I were in conversation. I had stopped thinking about how to focus. I just let it happen without really trying. As darkness gave way to light, the sights before me were too striking to behold. I saw five rings of fire. They were interlocking and looked like the Olympic rings. I heard the crackling sound of the fire on the circle's circumference. It was suspended in the air. Nothing could touch it. Nothing was holding it. Curiosity got the better of me. I had to know what it was.

"Counselor, what is that?" I asked in wonder.

"That's the Olympian symbol," Counselor responded casually.

"But what does it have to do with me? Why is it here in my heart?"

He knew I was eager to know the secret things. So, he went on, "You are an Olympian. You are in the race of your life, and you're here to win your race and finish the course. The winner isn't the one who comes first. The winner is the one who finishes the race. The way you run the race determines the experience you will have, and only you have the power to do that."

I had never thought of myself as a runner. In fact, I wasn't good at running. The Olympian rings of fire were alive in front of me like a vibrant glow. The more I gazed upon it, the more I began to feel like a runner in the deep part of my soul. I realized the darkness had disappeared and the light had consumed the Dark Room. I was transfixed. I hadn't noticed Counselor wasn't around until I looked for him.

"Counselor," I called.

There was no answer. There was no fear since he didn't seem to be there. My gaze returned to the rings of fire. There in the midst of the fire, was the face of Counselor. I gasped. He was the fire! I had never seen anything like it. He was my Coach, and he was training me to run in the race of life. I felt honored! What a revelation that was for me!

CHAPTER 7
Smooth and Slick

The stipend I was getting from the university wasn't enough for my monthly expenses. I decided to look for a part-time job on the weekends. A few blocks from the flat we lived in was a high-end store on West Street. One of the managers, Rob Moore, was from the same church I attended. Besides being a friend of my brother, Simon, our mothers were pretty close. I didn't know him too well. Whenever I bumped into him, either at church or on the street, we greeted each other. I needed a job, so I decided to give him a call.

Rob was quite pleasant and helpful. He recommended me calling a certain sales rep, who was looking for people to demonstrate keyboards. That sounded like something I would enjoy doing. Getting paid for playing keyboards was definitely a great gig. When I got up the next morning, the first thing I did was call the sales rep. After telling him a little about my background as a pianist, he employed me on the spot. I was absolutely thrilled!

Starting immediately, every Saturday I worked at the store demonstrating keyboards while completing my postgrad degree. Earning a decent wage gave me a sense of independence. That's when I decided to open a savings account. My dream was to attend a Jazz Orchestration program at a university in the United States.

During the holidays, I worked tirelessly every day. Since I earned a base salary plus commission, the latter being the greater portion, I tried to sell as many keyboards as possible. By the end of my first year, I was the top salesperson. Rob was thrilled that his store ranked the highest in keyboard sales.

A whole year had passed. We became somewhat friendly during that time, but not too close. One day when I walked into his office, we had a casual conversation that went on for a little longer than usual. It was easy conversing with him. Rob had the art of making people feel comfortable enough to open up to him; a true salesperson's gift. Something about the manner in which he communicated made people trust him. It was probably a combination of his soft tone, the pace at which he spoke, and his choice of words. Rob was smooth and slick. After twenty minutes into the conversation, he got up from his desk, walked over to his office door, and locked it. My heart began to beat out of fear. *Please don't let it happen again. Please. Please.*

By now, I knew the look of a man about to make advances toward a woman.

The atmosphere in his office changed in that moment, from one of easiness to awkwardness. Looking at me directly, he walked over to stand in front of me, took my face in his hands, and kissed me. I was so taken aback that I froze in disbelief for a split second. Not knowing how to respond, I succumbed. As my mind came to grips with what was really happening, I gently pushed him away. I use the word gently because I felt it would have been rude to be forceful. He must have misunderstood my gentleness because he came to kiss me a second time. I placed both my palms against his chest in an effort to halt him.

"Please don't do that again," I said shaking with low confidence.

Releasing me, he walked towards the locked office door, turned around and stood with his hands on his hips, facing me. With great confidence, he then proceeded to ask me an arrogant question.

"Did you enjoy that kiss?" He was so full of himself.

Standing there speechless, I felt trapped between Rob and the door; I knew I was cornered. My mind was saying *No* while my head was nodding in agreement. How could I offend him? I just couldn't stand up for myself. Living up to my character entirely, I played the nice game to appease him which was to my detriment.

Counselor was the only person who knew exactly how I felt. He knew my thoughts and he knew my heart. With Rob's arrogant question still reverberating in my head, I wasn't prepared for the next set of words he spoke. The most outrageous request gushed out of his mouth, splattering all over me. A request that was totally unbelievable and inconceivable!

"If you enjoyed that kiss, come over here," pointing to the floor right in front of him, "And you kiss me, then I'll let you go."

The nerve! His arrogance frightened me. His confidence rattled me. Being extremely shy by nature, I had never made the first attempt or move on a guy before. This was definitely something I didn't have the courage to do. Oblivious to the thoughts running through my mind, or maybe he had some idea what I was thinking, Rob stood there and waited patiently. Relentlessly, he continued to coerce me into kissing him. This must have lasted for almost half hour. Feeling like I was stuck in a time bubble, I thought the moment was never going to end. I picked up whatever courage I could muster, took a few slow steps in his direction until I was standing in front of him. Still unsure of myself, I stalled. His eyes softened in a way that felt somewhat safe. He was a master manipulator. Smooth and slick! I quickly lifted my lips to his, gave him a quick peck, and said,

"There."

The look on his face showed his dissatisfaction, followed by a comment,

"That's not good enough. Give me a real kiss."

It was so uncomfortable. I couldn't breathe. There was no excitement being kissed by a man the way it was portrayed in romance novels I had read. There was no safety in a man's embrace as depicted in the comfort of his strength. There was no sweet, heartfelt seduction to his words or loving tenderness in his eyes. Nor was there a sense of sincerity in his response. My thoughts jumped into a flurry of questions:

Is he going to keep me here until I give in? What would people be thinking about Rob and me alone in his office for such an extended period, especially with his door locked? How will I face the employees when I emerge from his office? What will they say about me? Will my reputation be ruined? How long will he persevere?

Rob didn't seem in any hurry to open the door or consider the repercussions of his actions. These wild thoughts gave me enough courage to kiss him again with a little more depth, and so I tried once more. Pulling me into his arms, he deepened the kiss ignoring my attempts to stop it. All the while, I kept telling myself, *This will never happen again.*

When he was satisfied, he stepped aside and allowed me to leave his office. I couldn't believe his boldness and confidence.

During the weekend, the whole kissing episode plagued my mind. I couldn't shake it. I almost wished I had his confidence. How did he do that? How come he was so assertive and had no feeling of remorse or guilt? His behavior was unpredictable. Unsure of what to expect on Monday when I got to work, I was on edge. A few minutes after I arrived, he came over to my desk and said with his signature soft tone,

"I'd like to take you out to lunch. Meet me at 12 p.m. outside 320 West Street."

There was no asking, just telling. Something about his commanding way fascinated me. I wished I could be that way. Although this sounds crazy, I was flattered. It was the first time a man wanted to take me out on a lunch date. George and I had always eaten at my parents' home. We had never gone to a restaurant together. I had read stories about lunch and dinner dates in books. It sounded romantic and intriguing, and so I agreed. When we met at the restaurant, he was the perfect gentleman. Pulling my chair out for me and allowing me to be seated before he sat down. The conversation flowed. In fact, it was quite pleasant. He was very warm and kind, making every effort to treat me like a lady. What a chivalrous man, I thought.

Lunch turned out to be delightful. To get to street level, we had to take the elevator down. It was empty. There was no one else but us. When the doors closed, he immediately pulled me into his arms and kissed me. I let him because I felt somewhat obligated especially since he treated me to lunch at a very nice restaurant. Rob sure knew how to romance a woman. If I weren't so naïve, I would have noticed just how good he was at this game. Strangely, I allowed myself to enjoy the moment, thinking I wasn't going to let this happen again. For two reasons: He was separated from his wife, and secondly, he wasn't the type of man I wanted. He wasn't a musician, he was tone deaf, and his dressing was old-fashioned. I couldn't see myself with him. The next day, he invited me for coffee after work, and I agreed yet again. I don't know why I did. Maybe because I didn't know how to say "Sorry, I'm not interested." That felt rude, so I went along. The more I said, Yes, the more difficult it was to say, No.

Three months had passed, and I realized I was in a relationship with Rob. None of my friends knew about him because I was embarrassed. Without realizing it, I was falling under his spell as he continued his slow and artful manipulation. Hanging out with my friends became a problem. He told me with who I could and couldn't hang out. He wanted me to relate every conversation I had with every guy I met. I felt like I was under constant investigation for a crime I didn't commit. Instead of feeling like the victim, I felt more like the guilty party. He had the uncanny ability to make me feel like I did something wrong even when I didn't.

I began second-guessing myself, wondering if there was any truth in what he was saying. Rob had tactfully pulled me into his world of mind games, and I didn't know the rules, so I lost every round. His possessiveness overtook him, and I became more and more fearful. To protect myself and stop the interrogations, I started to shade the truth about band practice at church.

One evening, my brother, Jonathan, and I, were on our way to church for practice. When we reached the front of our building, Rob was pacing up and down with his shirt open. He had a wild look about him that was terrifying. His expression was fierce, cold and accusing. His voice was gutturally hard unlike the one I knew, and he began threatening me. Jonathan wanted to say something to him, but I assured him I could handle it. I knew that wasn't true. Rob accused me of being sneaky and deceitful. He was right. I had lied to him. Even though I had done it to protect myself, the truth was that I lied.

Again and again, I took the blame. So, when he called me sneaky and deceitful, I believed him. Having no idea of normalcy in a relationship, I assumed that's how a relationship between a man and a woman worked.

Based on my distorted beliefs and my previous experiences, I chose to ignore the red flags flying aggressively in my gut. Whether it was ignorance or fear, I allowed myself to be manipulated. I was a willing victim, who thought she was guilty.

Fear became my friend, and its controlling power muted the voice of Counselor in my life. I lost sight of Counselor. Rob had taken up the space Counselor had once owned. Ignorantly, I relinquished rights to my voice. According to the Indian culture in Durban, a woman was expected to serve her man, and that's what I believed I was doing. Once again, my life was being governed by someone else, and I got to be the silent audience watching it all play out. I focused on all the nice things, hoping they would compensate for the not-so-good stuff. Stuff like when Rob opened the car door for me, or when he bought me expensive gifts or took me to romantic lunches and dinners. He did all those things to woo me.

Somewhere deep down, I thought Rob truly loved me and that's why he did what he did. He even listened to my stories, although a slew of judgments always followed them as he brought down his hammer of condemnation. He became suspicious of every man who even glanced my way in passing, whether we were in familiar places with people we knew or among strangers at the mall. Confused about what was right and what was not, I kept moving along, day after day, week after week, month after month, being afraid. Afraid of what? I don't even know. I had no idea. I was just scared.

It was Valentine's Day, and he wanted to do something special for me. As usual, he treated me to a romantic dinner, bought me a beautiful gold chain and expected the evening to end with me sleeping with him. He said he wanted to show me how much he loved me. I let it happen because I didn't know how to say No. While we were making love, images from the past came rushing into my thoughts. I didn't dare say anything to Rob for fear he would get angry with me or accuse me of thinking of another man, irrespective if that man was the perpetrator. I pretended everything was fine until I got home.

I went straight to the loo, locked the door, sat huddled in the corner on the floor, and cried my silent howl that I had mastered since I was a child. There will never be a man who could love me for who I am and treat my body kindly. I settled for less. It was the only option I had left. I knew I should speak to Counselor but the voice of Rob had become louder than Counselor's, and I didn't know how to adjust the volume.

Rob and his wife had been separated for a while before they started the divorce proceedings. His divorce was not finalized, and I was uncomfortable with that. It felt wrong, yet I couldn't do or say anything. I didn't have the guts to say anything. That's when Counselor's words rang in my ears,

"If the same thing happens Chloe, you can tell him not to touch you. I will be with you, but only you can say the words."

A glimpse of the Big Red Heart flashed before me. I longed to go to the Open Gardens, sit in its solitude, and have conversations with Counselor. I tried desperately to retrieve the images. I needed to see him. I had to find a way. Somehow.

Every time I wanted to say something to Rob, the words were stuck in my throat. He was commanding in his gentleness and manipulative in his loving. I continued to work at the store on Saturdays. His wife who was on leave had returned to work in the New Year, and I knew that was going to be very awkward for me. Although they lived separately, it bothered me that the divorce was still pending.

One Saturday morning, while he was in his office seated at his desk, I walked in, needing an answer to a work-related question. Five minutes later, his wife walked through the door. She headed straight in my direction, lifted her hand, and slapped me across my face. Rob got up from his desk, went over to her, held her arm as he led her towards the door. After a rough exchange of words between them, she left. He then turned to me and said,

"Don't breathe a word about this to anyone."

I couldn't believe my ears! So I said, "I'm going to report her to HR."

He responded angrily, "I want you to forget this whole incident ever happened. Do you hear me? You will say nothing to anyone. You better keep quiet. As far as we're concerned, this never happened. I will not lose my reputation and my job over this."

Disbelievingly, I stood there and said nothing. My fear levels shot up a few notches. I was a dumb prisoner who lost all rights to share my thoughts or try to speak up. I feared Rob. There was absolutely nothing I could do about it. Every time I thought about leaving the job, I remembered my dream to study Jazz in the USA. Music was far too important for me to take my eye off the ball. Living in fear and lacking the courage to communicate my point of view, I pretended like nothing happened. Retreating into my cocoon, I carried on living as usual, never bringing the subject up again. Rob was too powerful for me to fight back or say something. I feared him.

When things had subsided, I suggested that the both of us take a break. I tried a gentle approach to my argument.

"Your wife must want you back to do what she did. I don't want to stand in the way of a possible reconciliation."

They had only been married for about two years and had a son who was just a few months old. Reluctantly, Rob agreed.

"Okay, I'll try." This told me he was open to the possibility of getting back with his wife. Here was my escape, I thought! But to my disappointment, it was short lived.

A few weeks later, Rob began to pursue me relentlessly.

"I tried to make the marriage work, but it's not working out. It's over for good."

He was so convincing that I believed him, not questioning whose fault it could be. Looking back, it's hard to fathom how I couldn't see him for who he was.

We were back in a relationship whether I wanted it or not. I didn't have a say. Feeling stuck, I had to find a way to make the relationship work. Being a pleaser, I went along with whatever plans he had. Because I had lived a sheltered life, I felt there was nothing I could teach him. By default, he became my designated life tutor. My life lessons were his version of the truth. Rob's perspective on life and the lies he told me became the only truth I knew and understood about men and women. I couldn't draw comparisons because I had nothing to compare it with. He was my only point of reference. He sheepishly watched my every move, keeping a constant eye on me. I was afraid to speak to friends in case he suspected something was going on. He was always suspicious of everything and everyone. He always doubted people's intentions and chose to believe the worst. Through all of that, he came across as the sweetest and kindest man. Smooth and slick!

There were happy moments too. I chose to hold onto them rather than focus on the unhappy ones. Believing there is good in every human being, I gave Rob the benefit of the doubt. My rationale was this: If I showed him love and did whatever I could to please him, he would treat me well and wouldn't doubt me or accuse me. Maybe then he would become the man I believed he could be. What I didn't realize was that I had set a trap for myself and dug a deeper grave, a hole so deep, it wouldn't be possible to climb out of it. The changing and adjusting were one-sided. My side. This enabled him to continue his behavior, and it set the expectation for what was to come. Kindness, which was my greatest strength, had become my greatest weakness. Rob recognized that and proceeded to use it to exert complete control over me.

Something I always enjoyed doing was traveling with Prophet Zach and the band, sharing the gift of music and song. During the summer holidays, I worked every day. One day, I received a call from Prophet Zach, informing me that the team was invited to a series of weekend performances in Port Elizabeth. That was such exciting news! The whole band consisting of eight members would drive down together, hang out, have fun, and make beautiful music. After the call, I shared the news with Rob. Instead of being excited for me, he gave me a cold hard stare and said, "You're not going. If you go, then you're a loose woman. Unmarried women don't spend the weekend with men."

"But this is what we do. We play at different locations as a team. I have to go. Prophet Zach asked me to, and I agreed."

Rob retorted before I could complete my sentence,

"Call him back and tell him you can't go."

"But he'll want to know why I can't go, since I've already said yes."

"I don't care what you say to him. I'm telling you, you're not going anywhere, and you won't be going anywhere in the future. That's final."

Flabbergasted with his selfish response, my heart sank. How was I going to lie to Zach? He would know something's up. Being afraid of Rob, I made the call. Zach didn't believe me. He asked me over and over again why I wasn't coming. I said that something came up. He was so disappointed. Trying my utmost to hide my sadness, I told him,

"Zach, going forward, I won't be part of the team."

For a few moments, there was complete silence before he responded,

"Tell me what's wrong, Chloe."

"Nothing is wrong," I replied with a subdued voice.

He didn't want to accept what I was saying. He kept asking me what was wrong. I couldn't tell him the truth, but he knew. Because I was adamant, he finally gave in. I could hear the disappointment in his tone. The sharp, bright, upbeat voice of my mentor had lowered to a tone of surrender. When I put the phone down, I headed straight to the loo and cried my famous silent howl. Little by little, my life was being chipped away.

After his divorce was finalized, Rob began accompanying me to church. Everyone who knew me couldn't understand why I chose Rob. People often told me that Rob was not the right person for me. I smiled and told them what a nice person he was. Maybe if I said it multiple times, I would begin to believe it. I could make that into a truth. Because people loved me, they stood by me, supported my decision, and accepted Rob. My family and friends tried their best to make him feel welcomed, even though they were vocal about their displeasure with my choice. For me, it felt good sitting in church with someone by my side or even going places with him. Maybe this was due to my low self-esteem as a woman. Or maybe I liked having a masculine figure around. It gave me a sense of security in some warped way. Somehow it made me feel like a real woman in public. Probably because of my romantic delusions having watched too many Hollywood movies, and read too many romance novels.

My dress code was entirely different from Rob's style of dressing. He was old-fashioned and extremely conservative, whereas I was a funky dresser. Pins, leather, a few lobe piercings, short skirts and dresses, tight tees, ripped jeans, headbands, fashionable jewelry, all put together with a uniqueness that caught the attention of people. I apparently had my style of dressing which was entirely different from most people. But I liked being different. It somehow made me feel special and unique.

On a Saturday afternoon. Rob and I decided to go for coffee at a popular restaurant, which had the atmosphere of a diner. He walked ahead of me to a table of his choice. As we passed a table of about six guys, one of them complimented me. Rob caught something going on from the corner of his eye. Suddenly he swung around and came charging towards the guys, demanding to know who had made a comment. He began to scream and to cause a scene.

I stood there utterly embarrassed. This scenario had occurred quite a few times at different places. Although Rob was only six years older than me, I looked young for my age because of my petite frame. People mistook me for his daughter or his niece. Whenever he heard this comment, I knew that it upset him. He made every effort to correct the statement. With me, I was embarrassed for him and myself.

The way things were going, I shouldn't have been surprised when Rob made his next request. He wanted me to change my style of dressing.

"You need to start acting and looking like a lady," he retorted.

During one of the incidents, someone had mistaken me for his daughter. This prompted him,

"Do you know the reason why people are saying that? It's because you dress like a gypsy. Do you realize how comical you look with your choice of clothing and that ridiculous bag of yours?"

Thinking that he could be right, I believed what he said. Maybe if I dressed more sophistication, then I would look my age, and we wouldn't need to defend our relationship in public. So, I began to reform my style of dressing. One thing I knew for sure, I could never be a conservative dresser. I toned down my eclectic style to whatever the fashion sense was at the time.

More of Chloe was being chipped away. I was disappearing into the shadows, and a form of the woman Rob wanted me to be, began to emerge. A dark cloud came over me like a cloak, hiding the real person underneath. No Counselor, no music, and no Ama. Rob didn't even want me to spend time with my grandmother. He wanted me for himself only. I had sold myself to him and became a slave to her master. Maybe that's how life was meant to be. I didn't fight it, but gave in to the demands put on me. I wanted to be a good person, and in some twisted way, by giving myself up, I felt I was a good person. Sacrificing my happiness for the sake of someone else was a good deed in my eyes. I was generous, compassionate and kind. Those were wonderful traits to have as a woman. Inwardly, I felt a distorted sense of pride and accomplishment. I kept saying to myself,

Chloe is a strong woman with a big heart.

I had to believe it. I had to, otherwise, how was I going to survive. Suddenly a glimpse of something familiar slipped into my mind. It was the image of the Big Red Heart in the garden. It was as quick as a flash. I desperately tried to capture the images again, but I couldn't. I'd lost my way to Counselor, and couldn't find the path back.

Rob had taken over my thoughts, my smile, my happiness, my music, my character, my friends, and my family. There was nothing left for me except my piano. Whenever I sat to play, the notes were lifeless, the music was empty, and the pianist was soulless. It was all gone. All I had left was the version of Chloe designed by Rob. He got what he wanted, and I got to see a stage performance of a woman who looked like me, sounded like me, walked like me, but was someone else altogether. And I was part of the audience, with a front row seat, watching the show of a lifetime, and wondering how it will all end.

CHAPTER 8
A Musician's Dream

As a South African born jazz musician, my dream was to attend a music program in the USA. Mesmerized by the sounds of jazz, I had fallen in love with this fascinating art form. I learned about the evolution of jazz and the great artists who had transformed and mastered the art of improvisation and intricate chord structures. After researching jazz programs offered at music schools in the States, I decided to enroll in a Summer Program at the University of Rochester, Eastman School of Music, New York. I saved enough money to enroll in the Jazz Arranging Class. Although I desperately wanted to study Jazz Piano Master Classes too, I didn't have enough funds.

Once I received confirmation of my acceptance, my dad reached out to some of his friends to see if they knew anyone in the area who could provide accommodation. One of them referred us to a Lebanese woman who lived in a little town called Lima, an hour away from the university. After speaking to Martha on the phone, she willingly offered me a room for a three-month period. I had no idea how I was going to get from Lima to Rochester every day, and decided to cross that bridge when I got to it. Things were falling into place, and I couldn't believe my dream was coming true.

Rob was constantly upset with me. He couldn't understand why I had to stay for an extra month after my program. At the time, Delta Airlines offered non-US citizens a great deal; we could buy a thirty-day Delta Pass, and fly unlimited to any city in the States on standby, provided the ticket was purchased in the country of origin. The cost was $199. What an outrageous deal! The adventurous spirit inside of me loved exploring different places. I had to grab this deal-of-a-lifetime. The thrill of the unknown was enticing. I decided to throw caution to the wind and follow my free spirit. Some of my dad's friends were happy to have me as their guest for a few days. I decided to jet set around the States after the program.

Studying in the USA, even for a short period, was a dream I constantly spoke about to Rob before we started seeing each other. This subject was part of every conversation I had with family and friends. Everyone knew how I relentlessly pursued my American dream. Rob tried desperately to discourage me from going ahead with my plan, but thankfully it was on the table from Day One. My one non-negotiable! I guess if I had brought this up after we started seeing each other, it would have been shot down. Anyway, I don't think I would have dared to bring it up. It wouldn't have been possible. The week before I left, he refused to talk to me. He was angry. Although I was fearful, I wasn't going to let him take away the moment from me. It belonged to me.

The day had arrived. My bags were packed, and I was ready to fly away to another country by myself. No family, no friends, and no Rob. The taste of freedom was so close. I could smell it in the leather of my overnight bag. My dad had walked me through the journey; passport control, visas, travelers' checks, boarding passes. He even bought me a pink trip log to document my daily activities. I was all set. The day before, I had said goodbye to Rob, and I was grateful that was over.

Family and friends came to the airport to see me off, totaling about forty people. After my dad prayed for me, followed by tons of hugs, it was time. Picking up my overnight bag and my purse, I turned and walked away from everyone who loved me, wondering what lay ahead. Excited and anxious at the same time. Walking through security with confidence, recalling the step by step guide my dad had briefed me on. Everything went well. I completed my first mission successfully. The layover in Johannesburg was about three hours. It would give me enough time to check-in for my international flight to JFK airport in New York, go to the restroom, and stroll past the charming duty-free shops.

As I exited the plane and entered the domestic arrivals area, I couldn't believe who was waiting for me. Rob.

I was shocked and terrified! What was he doing here? What was going on inside his head? I didn't know what to think. Fear gripped me. I pretended to be happily surprised. The anticipatory feeling of excitement was immediately squashed. I had to play along. Not sure of his intention, I was on high alert. Was he going to stop me from leaving the country? Was he going to start an argument? Was he here to make me miserable before I leave in an attempt to destroy my happy moment? I waited to hear what he had to say.

"Surprised?" he asked with a small smile.

I smiled back nervously as I shook my head affirmatively.

"I wanted to surprise you because we didn't end on a good note yesterday," he said.

"I know," I replied, waiting to hear what else he had to say.

"I've been thinking," he paused for a moment, and then proceeded, "I've decided to come and join you at the end of your program so we can tour the States together. You don't have to do it alone."

He didn't ask me if I wanted him to join me. He informed me of his decision. Inside of me, anger began to arise, but I masterfully calmed it down. I knew him too well. If I dared to say No, he would have immediately accused me of being a loose woman, waiting to run around with men. I said nothing. I only listened. There was more. I knew that too. He always had some devious plot. I didn't know what it was.

"I have a great idea. Since you have extra money from your scholarship, why don't you pay for my airfare to New York," he continued, "And when we get back to South Africa, I'll give you the money." This was not a question. It was a statement.

That would deplete my funds, and I wouldn't have enough to complete my Master's program when I returned. Rob earned extremely well, at least five times more than my part-time wages. I wanted to ask him why he couldn't use his own money. I wanted to say, No, those funds are to complete my dissertation, travel costs to university and sundry expenses for the duration of my degree. I wanted to tell him to get lost. I wanted to scream and tell him to leave me alone.

Finally, I responded by nodding my head in agreement, accompanied by a small smile. He successfully manipulated me again, and coerced me into paying for his flight. I couldn't fight back. Here it was. He had the final word which put him back in control. I felt deflated and concealed my impatience to get away from him. It was time to check-in for my international flight.

"Okay. I need to check in now," I said softly.

"Don't worry. You have enough time," he replied, trying to stall me.

I had to force myself to say something otherwise I would miss my flight. It wouldn't have been a surprise if that's what he had planned all along.

"But I have to go. This is something I haven't done before. I want to give myself enough time in case something unexpected comes up," I said as I stood up, picked up my overnight bag, and looked in the direction of the gate. I purposely refused to look at him because I knew I would be intimidated by his menacing look. He waited until I slipped my bag over my shoulder, then accompanied me to the check-in line. After he kissed me, he said,

"Make sure you call me when you get to New York. I'll be waiting for that call."

I nodded. Smiling, I waved goodbye, as I walked further and further away from him. One last wave as I took the corner before I breathed a sigh of relief. Finally! It was an exhalation of the old bad air trapped inside my lungs impeding my ability to breathe freely and uninhibited.

Alone at last! It was heaven. Having the solitude of my own company was refreshing and liberating. For the first time in my life, I left behind everything that was familiar. No cultural restrictions, no family name to uphold, no religious dogma to adhere to, and no man to exert his control. The world awaited me. Pure delight and tranquility swept over me. Closing my eyes, I succumbed to the dawn of a new day.

Only he was there. I knew he would be there. Thousands of miles and high altitudes couldn't keep him away from me. Counselor was in my heart and my mind. I found myself strolling in the Open Gardens in front of the Big Red Heart. Glancing around, I noticed the flower buds starting to bloom. Gorgeous exotic colors waited to experience the touch of the sun on the skin of their forming petals. It's exactly how I felt inside, like springtime in my heart.

After many catnaps and shifting about in my seat for almost fifteen hours, I opened my eyes to behold the breathtaking New York City skyline in all its splendor. The pictures held in my mind came to life in 3D. From the elegant Statue of Liberty to the towering Twin Towers, from the steepled Empire State Building to the flickering lights of Times Square. My dream was no longer in my mind. It was right in front of me. It was real. I was in New York City! I couldn't wait to experience the spirit of this famous metropolis. A card with my name on it flashed in front of me as I exited security.

Dr. Ruth, a friend of my parents, had sent a gentleman to pick me up from the airport. As we drove through Manhattan, I was under a hypnotic spell. The people! They were everywhere. I couldn't believe it.

I spent three days at the home of Dr. Ruth. She was a stern looking black woman and welcomed me with an authoritarian tone. After piling food onto a plate, enough for three people, she invited me to sit at the table and eat the meal she had prepared for me. Just looking at the amount of food made me full. Slowly I dug into it. When I made it through a quarter of the meal, I said to her, "Thank you for lunch. I won't be able to finish my meal. I'm already full." She frowned and in a stern voice she said, "No one here wastes food. You need to eat everything on your plate."

Out of respect and gratitude, I sat and ate every grain on my plate, and it took me two hours to eat it all. I felt like a roly-poly. Thinking Dr. Ruth should be pleased with me, I asked,

"Can someone take me into the city today?"

She looked at me quizzically and answered,

"My dear, you're too tired. You need to take a shower and get to bed. Tomorrow Victor will come by and take you around."

Not understanding what she meant, I asked her,

"What do you mean by 'take a shower' Dr. Ruth?"

She looked at me as if I was talking gibberish and said, "Take a bath."

"Do you mean I should 'have a bath' or do you mean something else?" I asked for clarification.

A tiny smile appeared on her serious face, as she nodded, "Yes. I mean 'have a bath' Chloe." Thank God! She could smile. Dr. Ruth was right. I was tired, sleepy, and jet lagged.

The next day, by the time I got up, it was already noon. I couldn't believe I had overslept. I washed up and got dressed before heading downstairs to the kitchen. Victor, a Jamaican guy, probably in his thirties, was sitting in the living room waiting for me. As I descended the narrow staircase, he heard me and stood up. With a warm and friendly smile, he greeted me.

"Hello, Chloe. I'm Victor. How are you doing?"

"Nice to meet you, Victor," I replied. "I'm rested. Thank you for asking."

"We have a big day ahead of us. Why don't you grab breakfast so we can head out? Dr. Ruth asked me to show you around."

Hurriedly I gobbled down my cereal, anxiously waiting to see the sights I'd heard so much about from people, read about in books, and seen photographs taken by my parents when they visited.

"I'm ready to go," I said with my jacket in one hand and my purse in the other.

"Great! The subway is about a thirty-minute walk. Are you comfortable in those shoes?" he asked.

Confused, I answered his question with a question, "But aren't we taking the car?"

He looked at me surprised and let out a soft giggle.

"Chloe, this is New York City. Very few people drive cars here, besides the yellow cab drivers you see."

That day, I had my first subway experience. It was just like the movies. Totally surreal. As I emerged from the subway, I was blown away by the hustle bustle of the city. By the time we got to the Statue of Liberty, an hour and a half had passed. That was a long trip for me. In South Africa, traveling for more than forty-five minutes was a special trip. This was unbelievable! The lines were so long, we couldn't see where it began. It was almost two hours before we started our ascent. Beholding the beautiful views from the top, I was utterly entranced. Every aorta of exhaustion had magically disappeared. The views were spectacular! Scanning the skyline from one end to the other, I took in the splendor and the energy of New York City. We probably stayed at the top for about thirty minutes before we descended to take the ferry back to the mainland. It was almost evening.

Our next stop was the Empire State Building. Victor said, "The views of the city from the top of Empire State are gorgeous at night." He was right. When the doors of the elevator opened, I gasped in awe. It was magnificent and arresting. I stood there motionless and speechless. Everything in my life before that moment ceased to exist. There was no before or after. It was now. Victor interrupted my intoxicated state.

"Chloe, do you have the energy for one more stop? If you're tired, we can head back. Up to you." I was tired, but I didn't want to stop going so I said, "Let's keep moving." He smiled at my enthusiasm.

Next stop was Times Square. Nothing could have prepared me for the dazzling sensational experience of 7th Avenue and Broadway. The brilliance of flashing neon lights accompanied by the honking of horns and a chorus of spoken voices felt like I was inside a symphonic kaleidoscope. My brain was trying hard to absorb and understand this new world I was experiencing. I loved every ticking moment. If I could lengthen a second or hold back the hands of the clock, I would have done it. My first day in New York City was more than I had imagined. That night my mind was so stimulated, I couldn't fall off to sleep. I lay awake replaying the events of the day, before I slipped into Dreamland.

The next day, we visited the Central Park. The length of this beautifully landscaped park in the middle of New York City with ponds, restaurants and an ice rink was exquisite, like a quaint little town in a land of its own. I realized how small South Africa was in comparison to the United States. We had so much to learn and a long way to go. No wonder we were called a third world country.

After three days of experiencing the Big Apple, I was filled with excitement as I jumped onto the Amtrak heading for Upstate New York. I couldn't wait to arrive in Rochester. At the station, I was greeted by a petite middle-eastern woman,

"Chloe?"

Smiling, I nodded my head, "Yes. Are you Martha?"

"Yes. I'm Martha. Welcome! Nice to meet you," she said, giving me a warm embrace. She was kindhearted, and immediately I felt safe.

Rochester was so very different from the energetic vibe of New York City, yet it held a beauty of its own. The drive through the countryside to her home in Lima took about an hour. When we got there, she showed me to my room and suggested a short rest. After taking a shower, I wandered into the kitchen, feeling hungry, but too shy to say anything. She lifted her head and invited me to sit at the table, then served me a Mediterranean dinner. Afterward, she gave me a tour of her home and said, "Chloe, please make yourself at home. If you're hungry, help yourself to whatever is in the kitchen. I'm at the hospital most of the time so don't wait for me. Treat this as your home for the next three months."

Martha was a nurse, and her welcome was exactly what I needed. My spirit was rested and peaceful.

The bus stop was about a twenty-five-minute walk from Martha's house. There were only two buses that stopped in Lima on the way to Rochester, 6 a.m. and 7 a.m., too early for me since I was a late riser. Determined to see my dream turn into reality, I was up at 6 a.m. to be at the bus stop by 6:50 a.m., ready for the gift of a lifetime. Although Lima was a small town in the middle of nowhere, I was in America. In a few hours, I would be a music student at one of the top music schools in the country. It was euphoric.

The longest bus I had ever seen in my life, approached. It looked like an accordion. Fascinated, I sat in the seat situated in the rotating curve of the bus wondering how it would feel. South Africa didn't have buses this long. Gazing out of the window throughout the whole ride, taking in the countryside was refreshing. Everything felt brand new. Everything.

As the bus pulled into the Depot, my heart opened the door to what lay ahead. Counselor was there, waiting. As I got off, I walked in his direction, my eyes alight with expectation and delight. When I got closer, he disappeared into the crowds. Somewhere close, watching over me, was my protector and my best friend.

Eastman School of Music, University of Rochester, New York. I stood in front of the building and stared in wonderment. Could this really be happening? The space around me was vast and open. The air was crisp and clean. The streets were elegantly lined with exquisite designs. Inside the entrance hallway with its huge carvings and wooden floors, looked like a scene from a movie set. This was my dream come true. The old smell of antique and oak, surrounded my small frame. The walls had paintings of deep warm colors, making the humungous space feel cozy and homely. Straight ahead was a wide staircase with rich smooth-finished wooden banisters and big round knobs at the ends. It looked like a picture in a painting.

There Counselor was, waiting for me on the landing. Smiling. He seemed so happy to see me. Looking up at him, I realized just how much I had missed him. Making my way towards the bottom of the staircase, still keeping my gaze fixed on his face, I ascended the staircase, one step at a time in a slow, graceful glide. Somewhere inside the vault of my heart, I knew this was going to be a life-changing summer. The flowers were in full bloom, celebrating along with me. The colors splashed hope across my line of sight. I realized I was walking in my garden, suspended between two worlds. It was ethereal.

Glowing from within, I was drawn to the light in his eyes. I slowed my pace, even more, not wanting to rush the moment, but to savor the experience so I could carry it with me for the rest of my life. As I placed my right foot on the landing, he faded. Now was not the time for our conversations. He just wanted me to know he was there. I understood.

Glancing around, I found signs pointing to the registration office. As I walked along the corridors, looking for the office, I had the look of a contented young woman who had taken a warm, refreshing shower after many years. Nothing and no one could lay claim to my engaged senses, only the moment. A passion stirred inside of me beyond anything I had known before. A passion so deep and guttural that caused me to see my future self in blissful form. A beautiful earth-shattering experience. I was not dreaming. This was real. And Counselor was with me.

After registering, I wandered around the campus in awe, waiting to attend my first class. Ten students had signed up for Jazz Arranging. Because I was the only foreigner, everyone was intrigued including the instructor. New techniques and instrumentation, chord structures and voices opened my mind to a new way of composing and arranging. Sounds from different time periods and styles I'd never heard of, increased my thirst for more. Every lesson increased my capacity to listen and absorb a broader spectrum of sounds and textures.

One of the classes offered was on deconstructing a big band score to understand the elements and how they were used. As part of the requirement, the students had to conduct a high school band. That was something I had never really done before. Curiously, I slipped into the class and sat at the back, listening to the instructor guide the student as they conducted. Just observing that, made me nervous. I kept thinking to myself; I will never be able to stand in front of a band of that caliber and conduct from a score. It looked daunting. They were as good as the University big band back home.

At the end of the class, I went to the instructor and introduced myself. After apologizing for listening in without permission, I told him what a great opportunity American music students had. In South Africa, we didn't have the opportunity to conduct a big band. Firstly, there were no high school bands, and secondly, there were no courses that trained us to conduct bands. He was very surprised, especially when I mentioned that jazz was only introduced at the college level for the last three years. Whether it was out of compassion or kindness, I'm not sure. This is what he asked,

"Why don't you sign up for this class?"

"I would love to, but I don't have the money to sign up," I replied.

"You know what? You go ahead and sign up later today. I'm going to waive your fees," he said kindly as he rested his hand on my back reassuringly.

I was ecstatic and repeatedly thanked him, but also reminded him that I had no clue about conducting a big band. Settling my fears, he said,

"No worries. That's why I'm here."

At this point, I wanted to tell Counselor everything that had occurred. Instead, I walked over to the Jazz Arranging class to share the news with my instructor. He smiled at me and said,

"That's really great, Chloe. What other classes would you like to enroll in?" he asked.

"Jazz Piano Master Classes, but it's too expensive," I replied.

"Well, I'm the instructor for Jazz Piano. Let's set up two sessions per week for the whole summer," he offered.

"What? Are you sure?" I asked disbelievingly.

Smiling from ear to ear, he nodded and said, "Yes, Chloe. I am sure. We can start tomorrow."

This dream was turning into another dream. It felt surreal, like a dream within a dream. As I walked away, the ground felt like I was walking on air. My mind was swirling around in utter amazement. People always talked about the American dream. That's precisely what it felt like to me.

At the same time every evening, Rob called me when I got back to Lima. Although I went along with whatever he said, I didn't share my good news with him. Some nights, I stayed over at my friends' place in Rochester. Not wanting to create unnecessary problems, I came up with a valid excuse in advance.

"Martha is working a long shift tomorrow so she asked for peace and quiet in the evening. Please don't call because I won't be able to speak to you. I want to respect her request."

He didn't like it, but having no option, he irritably gave in. Every time I used the same excuse. I was careful not to aggravate him in case he showed up on Martha's doorstep.

Rob was eager to give me the details of his flight. Pretending I was happy to hear it, I wrote down the information grudgingly. He was too far away, and I didn't care. Although speaking to him on the phone felt like a duty I was forced to fulfill, nothing he did or said had the power to crush my spirit. I was on top of the world, and loving every moment of it.

At night, as I lay on my bed, replaying the events of the day, I eased into a welcoming bed of joy and satisfaction. Somewhere in my reminiscing, Counselor faded in. I exhaled in total surrender and completeness. It had been so long. Although I had so much to say, my words were the sound of silence. I stayed. I rested. I renewed. I reset. I revived. I was home. That night I slept like a baby. Deep and peaceful without a worry in the world. Completely at rest.

My days at Eastman School of Music were unforgettable. I learned linear jazz arranging. I learned drop two chord voicings. I learned how to conduct big bands. I learned how to listen for entry points of different instruments and cue them in. I learned how to arrange for and conduct a one-hundred-piece orchestra. I learned jazz piano techniques, unusual voicings, and comping. I listened to and immersed myself in live jazz a few times a week. I hung out with friends until all hours of the morning, without fear of curfews and house rules. I laughed freely and talked openly. I heard interesting stories of my fellow students who had become friends. I saw how unique their journeys had been and how different they were to mine, growing up in South Africa. I stayed over at friends' places, not needing to ask for permission to do so.

Contented with life, I closed my eyes restfully as I sat in the accordion bus on the way back to Lima. Everything seemed perfect and beautiful. My heart and my thoughts were in total synchronicity when an old familiar sensation warmed my heart.

"Chloe, I've missed you," came from somewhere deep inside of me.

Suddenly I longed to visit the Big Red Heart. It began to tug at my heart. He was waiting for me. I had to see him. I had to talk to him.

"Counselor," I breathed.

At last, I could hear him. There were no other distractions, no other noises, and no other voices.

"I've missed you too. I couldn't hear you, Counselor. I tried but I just couldn't," wondering how I survived for all this time.

"What matters right now is that I'm here with you," he offered comfortingly.

Stretching out his hand toward me, he invited me, "Come Chloe. Let's go."

The pitter-patter of my flapping valves transported me to the world of a cheerful little girl. I found myself standing under a graceful pastel waterfall that sprayed mist on the gardens. I felt the soft droplets on my face, my skin, my hair, my clothes. Lifting my hands to clear the water from my face, baffled me because it was not wet. Instinctively I touched my hair to feel the weight of the water, but it was completely dry. How could this be possible? I felt drenched in this dazzling waterfall and knew it defied the element of its nature.

Looking at Counselor through the mist quizzically, I opened my mouth to ask the inevitable, and caught him laughing at me.

"Why are you laughing? What's so funny?" I looked for answers.

"You," he said as he continued to smile, "You've forgotten. In our world, nothing makes sense. It's a world where the impossible is possible. Don't you remember?"

That was so true! I had forgotten that everything about Counselor and me was different. I burst out laughing until the both of us had fallen on the grass, rolling in the open fields of beauty. Oh my! I didn't want it to end.

"The next stop is Lima," I heard the announcement.

Awaking, I smiled and said to myself, Home. I'm home at last.

CHAPTER 9

An Interrupted Dream

My days at Rochester had come to an end. The Jazz Arranging program was over, and it felt bittersweet. I had the time of my life and wished I was doing it all over again. On the last night, the music students decided to have a final get-together. Friends I had made over the summer pitched up at the little studio where the party was being held. It was one of the many nights of fun, chatter, and music. We talked, laughed and shared stories about our hot summer days until the early parts of the morning. Some students had fallen off to sleep wherever they could rest their heads; some kept on talking, while others started to leave one by one.

It was mid-morning, time to say goodbye. We hoped we would see each other again someday, but I knew that was the last time for me. After being showered with hugs, I headed back to Lima. Although it was sad to part ways, carrying beautiful memories in my heart somehow made it easier. My days at Eastman School of Music will never be forgotten. I finally understood the phrase: Living the dream. It was as real as flesh and blood. The surge of life ran through my veins, and I felt wonderful.

I still had a whole week in Lima before heading back to New York City. During my three-month stay, I attended a church about ten minutes from Martha's home. April, the Music Director, was a talented pianist. We had gotten close during my time there. She had an insatiable desire to pursue a degree in Music, so she found every opportunity to hang out with me.

Canandaigua, a quaint town about thirty minutes east of Lima, was home to the Finger Lakes Performing Center, which was in an open park setting along Canandaigua Lake. I found out that Dave Brubeck was on the weekend schedule. What an amazing coincidence! He was the father of Darius, my Jazz Studies teacher, and mentor. I asked April if she was interested in going with me. Of course, she jumped at the chance.

The excitement was oozing out of me. I couldn't wait to see, hear, and experience this jazz legend perform. We left early enough so we could get a good spot, since there were no assigned seats. As we drove along stretches of open green fields, April asked me all sorts of questions about Dave Brubeck. The views on the way to Canandaigua were spectacular. Suddenly, the scene transformed into something divinely created; Canandaigua Lake lay peacefully between two luscious mountain slopes touched by earthy shades of autumn. It was breathtaking! I gasped in wonder,

"Beautiful," I murmured.

"And peaceful," I heard April respond.

Nodding in agreement, I was captivated by the glorious creation of God's earth. Opening the window with a slow, smooth movement as not to disturb the silence of the moment, I allowed the gentle breeze to brush against my face with fresh strokes. I had never seen the magnificent colors of autumn leaves except in pictures; a perfect combination of browns and oranges displayed in shades that could only be blended by a skilled master of the arts, accentuating the tranquility of the lake. That's why there is a song called 'Autumn Leaves.' This scene deserved a song title.

After paying our entrance fees, we made our way to the front section of the park and sat in a spot where we had a full view of the piano keys. Hungry and excited, our tummies began to rumble. While I secured our seats, April got us some hot dogs, sodas, and snacks from the food stand. I felt like a star-struck giggling schoolgirl anxious to experience the sensational music of a jazz icon.

"Chloe, are you going to try to talk to him after the concert?" April asked.

"I don't know. Let's see if we can get close enough to get his attention," wondering if it was even possible.

A very tall man entered and gracefully made his way to the piano. You could feel the excitement in the crowds as they applauded in celebration. He took his seat at the piano. Turning towards the audience, he smiled with a gentleness that was strikingly familiar. Darius was the spitting image of his father! The cheering of the crowds softened to a tender silence. Dave Brubeck placed his hands on the keys, and I held my breath. Clean, crystal notes floated across the open park charging the air with vibrant life. He played with a fluidity that captivated every person, taking us under the spell of his enthralling music. The opening lines for two of his famous tunes, 'Blue Rondo a la Turk' and 'Take Five' triggered a display of excitement across the audience. Its notable rhythms were mesmerizing. I didn't want the music to stop, but I knew the concert was coming up to the finale.

After the thunderous clapping and whistling, the thrill of the encore left me feeling satisfied and fulfilled. As Mr. Brubeck got up and walked off the stage in the direction of the artists' vehicle, the media surrounded him. People rushed from every direction, wanting to get his autograph. Security had to control the crowds. I thought to myself; there's no way I'll be able to talk to him. Suddenly a deep reverberating guttural sound emerged as I shouted out, "I'm from South Africa. I know Darius."

He stopped dead in his tracks, swung around, and asked, "Who said that?"

I flagged my hands wildly trying to get him to see me since I was only five feet tall. Brubeck, on the other hand, towered over most of the people surrounding him. His eye caught my flagging movements.

Reaching into the crowd, he grabbed my hand, and firmly but gently guided me into the artists' vehicle. I quickly said, "I'm here with my friend."

"Where is she?" he asked.

When I pointed to April, he beckoned her to get in with us. Mr. Brubeck had his eyes fixed on me. He was so excited. As soon as we pulled off, he asked, "Tell me about my son. How is Darius?"

I told him Darius and his wife Cathy were doing well. I told him that Darius was not just my jazz piano teacher, but he was also my lecturer in every subject since I was specializing in Jazz Studies. He wanted me to keep talking about his son. He asked about the work he was doing in South Africa. I told him what a tremendous impact Darius had made in South Africa in a short space of time. We drove to a small building just a few yards away. It was apparently the artists' lounge area. He ushered us in and offered us something to drink. The place was packed with musicians and media folk. Cameras were flashing, and reporters with big microphones wanted to interview him, but he redirected them to me as he said, "Talk to Chloe from South Africa. She's a student of my son Darius."

They proceeded to interview me. With astonishment, I responded to their questions. I don't even remember the questions nor my responses. I couldn't believe what was happening. What an unforgettable day!

About thirty minutes later, Mr. Brubeck was ready to leave. He wished me well, said goodbye, and hugged me.

"Tell Darius I miss him," he said with a softness in his eyes.

I nodded and assured him I would as I hugged him back. Such a memorable moment! On the ride back to Lima, April and I couldn't get over what had just occurred. It was like a dream.

That night I lay in bed, replaying the moments of the day with my eyes closed, I found myself browsing in the Grace Room. It was filled with gift boxes of all sizes and shapes, bookshelves of masterpieces, bottles of oils and fragrances. I noticed some of the gift boxes were empty, some of the books were left open on tables, and some of the bottles of fragrances were half-filled. Along the length of the wall, was a live painting of the earth. It lit up wherever my glance landed. Hundreds and thousands of people the size of little dots busily moved around. There were cars and buses, streets and houses; the cities were alive.

In other places, I saw towns and villages with a handful of people strolling along seemingly without a care in the world. Although I couldn't see their faces, I felt the energy come off the map. Totally fascinated, I slipped into a deeper daydream wondering what it all meant. I knew Counselor would reveal the mystery of the living map.

"Chloe, come over here," I heard him call me.

Following the sound of his voice, I saw him sitting on the garden swing. He tapped the tiny space next to him. As I sat close to him, he said with a faraway look in his eyes, "Fascinating, isn't it?"

He was deep in thought. I didn't want to interrupt him. I just watched. He already knew what was going through my mind.

"You saw empty gift boxes, right?" I nodded.

"Those gifts are now active in you. Think about how you've grown from the first time you entered the Grace Room."

That was a fact. I was a whole new person. So much had changed in me. I grew up!

"But why are the books strewn all over on the table?" I asked.

"Because those are the chapters of your life you're living right now. It reveals your purpose as it unfolds little by little, masterpiece by masterpiece, day by day." He turned to look at me and to gauge how I was responding to all of this.

"Why are the bottles of fragrances and oils half-filled?" was my next question.

"What do you think has been healing the wounds of your heart? That is the salve that has been repairing the cracks of your heart."

This was mind-blowing! I could see the whole picture coming together miraculously. Until Counselor showed me how much I had grown, and where I'd come from, it didn't hit me before that moment. Looking back, I could see the pieces fit together in one continuous flow as I had seen in the Design Room.

"One more question," I said.

"I know," he said, and then his gaze began to drift again. That was the first time I had experienced this distinctive scene. I was intrigued! But I knew I was about to find out.

"This beautiful world right here," motioning his hands across the whole garden with ease, "is your heart."

Anxious to hear what he was going to say next, I kept watching him.

"Inside your heart resides the whole world." Pausing for a moment, he continued, "That living map is your heart."

He waited as though he was breathing deeply. I had no words. The mystery was too great. Could it be what I thought it could be? Could it be that Counselor resides in me and I reside in him? Could it be that I am inside the living map with the rest of the world? And if the whole universe resides in his heart, then how big is his heart to carry all of us? And does each person carry the entire world in their hearts too? Who is this magnificent being that baffles me every time he reveals a new mystery? Will I ever get to fully understand the magnitude of his intelligence and the depth of his love? Life was bigger than me. Everything in life was interconnected at numerous levels. It was an ecosystem layered with complexities, too great for the human mind. To comprehend this phenomenon would be to live in the great unknown.

As human beings, I realized we lived in both worlds. Some of us enjoyed the unknown element of life, while others preferred to live in the know. I realized how fascinated I was by the unknown. It held an element of surprise and wonder for me, yet there was anxiety about its uncertainty.

"You received a big part of the mystery today, Chloe. Are you ready for the next chapter of your life?"

"As long as you're with me Counselor, then I'm ready."

It was time to leave Lima and say goodbye to Martha, April, and friends in the community. Another farewell moment! I didn't expect to make so many friends. Such a precious time! So many memories! So many lessons learned! So much growing up within just three months! My evolving heart was complete. It was one of the best times of my life. As I got on the Amtrak to head back to New York City, my heart began to beat to a strange rhythm. "What is this?" I asked myself as I sat on the train.

"Fear," came the answer.

Counselor knew.

Rob was arriving in the afternoon, and I had ample time to get to the airport to meet him. To my surprise, the cab from the station to the airport took much longer than I had anticipated. It was my first experience sitting in a car in New York City traffic from Grand Central to JFK airport. There was no way I could have taken the subway. My luggage was too heavy. The longer I sat in the cab, the more anxious I became. He would have arrived an hour ago. Fear rose in me at a steady rate. My hands were sweaty. My breathing quickened. Impatiently, I kept looking at my watch hoping the minute hand would obediently slow down. He was going to be furious.

Instead of reaching out to Counselor, Rob had consumed my attention in the flick of a moment. The fear shut me down and dragged me unwillingly back to being the familiar prisoner. After what seemed like an eternity, we arrived at the airport. Hurriedly I paid the cab driver, carried my large suitcase in one hand and my overnight bag in the other, and made my way through the terminal doors. The crowds were overpowering. Standing on tiptoes, I tried to spot Rob. He was nowhere to be seen. Rushing over to the airline information desk, I queried if his flight had arrived.

"Over an hour ago," came the reply.

I could feel my chest constricting. Where could he be, I wondered?

"I'm expecting someone, but I don't see him anywhere. Do you know where I could find him?" I asked, knowing it was a ridiculous question. How could she know Rob's whereabouts?

"You may want to check the Ground Transportation area," she offered, pointing in the direction.

As I got closer, I saw him pushing his way forward to talk to the attendant.

"Rob!" I called out loudly over the crowd.

Turning his head, he saw me and made his way over.

"Why are you so late? Do you know I arrived over an hour ago?" he asked angrily. "Who were you with?" he asked accusingly.

Here we go again! I thought to myself. No hello. No kiss. No hug. No "I'm happy to see you." Just his usual self after three months apart. Although he had a smaller bag, he didn't offer to carry mine. We walked over to the taxi without another word spoken. Feeling miserable, I followed obediently.

"The traffic was terrible," I said in my defense. "I didn't realize it was going to be that bad."

He just ignored me and looked out of the window. Withdrawing into my corner, my days in Rochester felt like decades ago. When we got to the hotel, he took a shower and went straight to bed. That was the first night we slept together in the same bed. I cringed thinking what my parents would say if they knew. I felt dirty and unclean even though nothing physical had happened.

Moving quietly, I lay down on the bed on the far end. I stayed awake all night, while he snored. I didn't stay awake because of his snoring; I stayed awake because I was afraid.

The next morning, he shot me a load of questions, more like an interrogation. He wanted information; where I'd been, who I was with, what did I do, etcetera. There was suspicion in his eyes and accusation in his tone. I could read him like a book. I tried to be as honest as possible, leaving out specific bits of information that I thought would trigger him, even though I had done nothing wrong.

After checking out of the hotel, we made our way to the airport to activate our Delta Passes. Deflated and excited at the same time, we decided our first stop would be Boston. I was anxious to see Berklee School of Music, the Number One school for Jazz.

Boston was gorgeous. Parts of the city reminded me of Rome with its cobblestone streets. After dropping off our luggage at the hotel, we hopped onto a bus with our first stop being Berklee. It was beyond my wildest expectations. I kept saying to myself, "I'm finally here."

I'd read about it in the Jazz magazines Darius had subscribed to for the students. I'd heard my fellow jazz musos talk about it regularly. It was every aspiring jazz musician's dream. Just being there was enough for me.

Afterward, we took the Boston Duck Tour, hitting all the main sights and attractions, then ending the day at Quincy Market by the river. It was all quite an experience. The atmosphere was vibrant with shoppers' chatter and laughter, street performers, and the cool jazz of Miles Davis' floating in the air, luring me towards it. Crowds of people gathered around the bandstand. Refreshing sounds of 'Blue in Green,' a favorite Davis standard, filled the open marketplace.

Rob and I found seats close to the front. As soon as the band took a break, I walked over to the keyboard player to compliment his playing. He was appreciative. We spoke the language of music and shared our musical experiences. Both of us listened intently to each other, as we chatted about different cultures with their unique sounds and rhythms. He was fascinated by the wonderfully complex rhythms of Africa. All the while, Rob sat watching me. When I got back to the table, he glared at me and made an outrageous statement,

"You're a loose woman, walking up to a strange man and talking to him."

I stared at him not knowing how to respond. Here we go again. After reflecting for a moment, I actually started thinking, maybe he is right. According to Durban Indian culture, it was probably true. Being away for a few months had set me free to be a true performing artist. I connected with like-minded people without inhibition.

Rob was furious and didn't speak to me for the rest of the day. We headed straight back to the hotel. The evening was bleak and silent. He watched television for the rest of the night while I slept.

The next day we flew to New Orleans, the birthplace of Jazz. It was fascinating! Jazz on Bourbon Street, a boat ride through the bayou across the Mississippi River, ending the evening at Preservation Hall in the French Quarter. The entry fee was only one dollar. Darius had recommended going there to listen to traditional jazz. The line was wrapped around a few blocks, and the wait time was about a couple of hours. We hoped we would be able to catch the last bus back to the hotel, which was across the river. It was getting dark. By the time we got to the door, it was inevitable we weren't going to make it in time for the bus.

"I'm here, and there's no way I'm not staying to listen to live jazz in this famous place," I thought to myself. Then I said to Rob, "We should stay since we're right here. We don't know when we will have the opportunity to come back again. We can always figure out a way to get back to the hotel."

He agreed with me, and I was glad. When we got into Preservation Hall, I was surprised by the small space. There was no air-conditioner, limited seating and standing room, and everyone was tightly squeezed together. No one cared about the space. Everyone enjoyed the ambiance and the experience. The sounds of traditional New Orleans jazz were real, raw, and riveting. Nothing could have prepared me for this time capsule adventure.

After the set ended, we stepped back into the present world and realized we had no idea how we were going to get back to the hotel. Making our way to the bus station, we decided to catch any bus that took us across the river and then we could grab a cab. During the day, we had asked the locals about getting back. All of them warned us of the dangers that existed if we didn't take the right bus. I guess if you haven't experienced the real danger, then there was no reason to be afraid.

An Interrupted Dream

It was 11 p.m., the day before my birthday. I definitely didn't want to be lost or face danger for the first few minutes of my birthday. Most of the bus drivers said there was only one way to get across. They warned us it was dangerous and we needed to get a cab as quick as possible because we would be in the Project. We had no idea about the Project. Anxiety began to creep in. Why was everyone warning us about impending dangers in the Project?

We got onto the bus. It was half empty. There was dead silence except for the running engine. As soon as we crossed the river, darkness surrounded us. Fear set in. People jumped off at different stops. About forty-five minutes had passed. I turned around to see how many people were still on the bus. There were four of us; the driver, a black male with a white coat sitting in the last row, Rob and me. We arrived at the final stop. As we got off, the bus driver said with a concerned look,

"Walk as fast as you can along this road until you come to the gas station. There you'll find a phone booth. Call a cab immediately. Don't hang around here. People don't come out of this area alive. Be careful."

By now, I was terrified. I kept praying for safety. The third gentleman also stepped out of the bus. He looked calm. In a warm and safe tone, I heard him say,

"He's right. Follow me," as he led the way, "and walk quickly."

It was pitch black. Not a person in sight. Not a vehicle in sight. Just bushes on either side of the road. All we could hear was the crunch of our shoes on the tarred road and the eerie sounds of insects at night. We walked swiftly without uttering a word until we got to the gas station. The man took us to the phone booth and waited until we called the cab. Rob said,

"The cab will be here in ten minutes," and the man nodded his head.

Ten minutes felt like ten hours as the minute needle moved past midnight. It was my birthday! I felt God was punishing me because I was with Rob.

"What a way to start your birthday!" Rob said.

Without commenting, I silently prayed for God to protect us. I called on Counselor to help me. We were standing in a hidden area, so no one passing by would spot us. Headlights were coming in our direction, and the vehicle began to slow down. We first waited to see if it was the cab before we emerged. It was! Thank God! We turned around to thank the man in the white coat, but he had disappeared. He was nowhere to be seen. My heart pounded as fear and anxiety turned into something else. I can't describe what I felt, whether it was a different kind of fear or apprehension. A sense of the supernatural lingered as we jumped into the cab. Rob and I looked at each other, shocked,

"He had to be an angel," I said.

Rob nodded his head in agreement. There was no other explanation. God had protected us. When we got to the hotel, I breathed a sigh of relief before falling on my knees and thanking God for his divine protection. That night I couldn't sleep. My thoughts were in a state of wonderment. An awesome fear of being in the presence of a celestial being overcame me. Drifting off to sleep in the early parts of the morning, I knew we were going to have a late start. By the time we got up, it was noon. Rob gave me a birthday card which displayed a list of famous people who shared the same birthday as me. A notable person was Michael Jackson.

Rob took me for breakfast. He was overcompensating probably because of the incident the night before. For the first time, he asked about my studies and experiences at Eastman. Trusting him and feeling safe especially after what had happened a few hours earlier, I willingly began to tell him the tales of my days in Rochester. I had journaled everything in the Pink Travel Log dad had bought for me. Taking it out of my bag, I paged through it, recollecting and relating all the fantastic things that had occurred and people I had met. Rob put out his hand and said,

"Let me read it."

And I gave it to him to read! I had forgotten this was the same suspicious Rob that misconstrues and misinterprets everything he sees, hears, or reads. My birthday had turned into hell!

He was silent for the rest of the afternoon. I could feel the tension building up. I knew something in my journal had triggered him. I couldn't think of what it was. He slipped my Pink Travel Log into his pocket, and I was afraid to ask for it. By the evening, I pretended to sleep while he watched television with the log on his bedside table. Fear began to overtake me. I didn't know if this fear was worse than the traumatic experience of being in the Project. I must have fallen off to sleep after quite some time. Suddenly, I was awakened by someone roughly shaking me. Getting up, I turned around and looked at him questioningly, wondering what was the matter.

With a hard, cold tone, he said,

"Get up! Don't think I'm going to let you sleep when I know what you did."

What I did? What did I do? Why was he so wicked? What kind of love is this?

"I don't know what you're talking about," I said calmly. Pushing my Pink Travel Log in my face, he said,

"This! Do you think I can't read between the lines? How many men did you sleep with?"

Vile, horrible words spewed out of his mouth. He left no space for me to respond. I couldn't say anything or explain anything. He refused to listen. Judgment was passed, and there was no trial. This was my birthday! I turned away and closed my eyes. He poked my back aggressively with his finger,

"Get up and sit up. You're not sleeping tonight until you admit what you did."

He kept me up the whole night, hounding me while I cried and sobbed uncontrollably and asked for his forgiveness for whatever he thought I did. There was no way out. With whatever courage I could muster, I got off the bed, got dressed, and sat outside the hotel room door on the floor. I cried the whole night wishing I was dead. I realized that even though I wished I was dead, I didn't want to die because I had Counselor. He gave me every reason to live. He was always with me, and I held the mystery in my heart.

Rob never came to get me or find out how I was doing. He heard me cry through the night. That pleased him because I was miserable. The behavior of a narcissist! About 7 a.m., I went back inside. He was asleep. I crept into bed slowly so he wouldn't know. That was the first of many horrible birthday experiences with Rob.

After New Orleans, we made our way to Michigan where I was scheduled to meet a Music Professor from the University of Michigan in Ann Arbor. The prior year, Professor Jim had spent a year at the University of Kwa-Zulu Natal as a Visiting Professor. During one of our long conversations, he asked me about my Master's dissertation. I told him it was based on the jazz opera *Porgy and Bess*. Excitedly, he explained that the original Porgy, Todd Duncan and the original choral director, Eva Jessye, lived in Michigan and he knew the both of them very well. They were connected to the University. He knew I would be visiting the US and so he asked me,

"Would you like to interview them for your research? I could set it up."

"Yes, that would be wonderful."

Professor Jim and his wife Carol were waiting for us at the airport in Ann Arbor. They were thrilled to see me again. I had written to him in advance to say I was coming with my fiancé. It was a lie, but I didn't know what else to say. They took us for lunch before dropping our bags off at the hotel. He told me he had set up the interview with Todd Duncan that afternoon, and Eva Jessye for the next morning. So many beautiful things were happening in my life, except for one thing - Rob.

Staying on an upbeat note, Rob and I headed to the interview with the original Porgy. Because I had started researching 'Porgy and Bess' over a year ago, I knew the opera and its structure very well.

A six-foot-tall light-skinned man, probably in his early nineties, stood with stature and elegance as he opened the door and welcomed us into his home with a booming voice.

I can only imagine what he sounds like when he sings, I thought.

Duncan was a classically trained baritone and had played the role of Porgy more than 1800 times. He was George Gershwin's personal choice. He invited us to sit down and offered us something to drink. I had prepared questions ahead of time and proceeded to interview him. He took my breath away as he walked me through his journey as Porgy from the moment he first met George Gershwin. I was in awe, and so honored to be speaking to him.

At the end of the interview, he stood up, and sang, *I Loves You Porgy*, followed by *Bess You is my Woman*. It was breathless! To hear it sung by the voice, I had heard so many times on the recordings, was truly magical. The beauty of his voice as it resonated through his home was tremendous. After the interview, he bent down and kissed me on the cheek. I thanked him and returned his warm smile, as he held my small hand between both his large hands. It was warm and heartfelt.

Professor Jim said, "Chloe, the next day is going to be a full day."

In the morning when he picked us up, we headed straight to Eva Jessye's home. She was a vibrant woman with eyes that were alert and curious. She asked me all sorts of questions about South Africa. I kept wondering who was interviewing whom. It felt like I was being interviewed. Smiling to myself, I recognized that she was bold, extroverted, and had a fearless spirit.

I pulled out my list of questions and started with the first question. Her response was unending. She didn't leave any details out. She answered every question thoroughly. She loved having company yet I could tell she was a no-nonsense person. She looked like she took control and got things done with excellence. On a little table next to her, she picked up the Playbill for *Porgy and Bess* and gave it to me,

"I want you to have this," she said.

My heart was filled with gratitude. About an hour-and-a half later, we left. I hugged her and thanked her for her graciousness. Professor Jim took us to the University of Michigan, which was close by. He said,

"You have to see the University. It's an Ivy League."

I didn't understand the big deal until I stood outside and looked upon this remarkable structure. What a glorious sight to behold! The architectural design wrapped with ivy was out of a storybook. The Music Department was gorgeous in architectural beauty and design, exquisitely manicured lawns that stretched across the campus, surrounded by peaceful lakes. After a comprehensive tour, he said we were going to take a drive to Lake Erie.

Professor Jim really went out of his way to entertain us. A kind generous man with a big heart. Lake Erie was the largest lake I had seen. He pointed to the other side of the lake and said, "That's Canada."

We stood and took in the fantastic views. I tried to hold the scenes in my mind so I wouldn't forget this experience. I felt blessed and favored. We had dinner right across from the lake at one of the restaurants. When Rob got up to go to the restroom, Professor Jim said in a fatherly tone,

"Chloe, I'm glad we have a quick moment to talk. What are you doing with this man? He's too old and conservative for you. You're a talented and gifted young lady. You have a bright future ahead. Are you sure this is what you want? Don't jump into any decision without thinking this through. I'm really concerned about you. When I saw him at the airport, I was taken aback."

There was nothing I could say to him. He saw right through the farce. I sat there dumbfounded.

"I know what you mean. I don't know how this is going to end. When we get back to South Africa, I'm hoping things sort itself out."

He could see the hopelessness in my eyes, and he assured me of his support with whatever decision I made. This was yet another warning! I didn't know if I had the courage to address this whole messed up relationship. As Rob approached the table, we changed the subject. Those few days in Ann Arbor with Professor Jim and his wife Carol were terrific.

The time had come for me to fly back home. Rob decided to stay for two more weeks on an airfare I paid for with my scholarship money. It made me bitter, but I said nothing. He casually told me,

"Since I'm in the States, I'm going to travel and do some sightseeing."

Too afraid to question him, I nodded my head in acknowledgement.

Saying goodbye at the airport couldn't come and go fast enough. As I turned and walked away from him, my heart and my mind had already gone ahead. I couldn't wait to get two weeks of relief. What kind of life was this? What did he want with me? It was clear he didn't love me. If you love someone, you don't treat them that way or make them feel worthless. I had to decide. It was up to me and no one else.

Getting back to South Africa felt like freedom because Rob wasn't there. I convinced myself the relationship was over and I would tell him so when he gets back.

Two weeks later, I got a call on the day he arrived. He wanted to meet me. I needed to tell him it was over. I said to myself over and over,

Chloe, you have to do it. You have to break off the relationship. You have to tell him you can't live with someone who is so suspicious and condemning.

Counselor's voice kept ringing in my head,

"I'll be with you, but only you can say the words."

The day had come. The moment had finally arrived. I was geared up and ready. I could see him standing and waiting. Fear began to rise inside of me, as I walked toward him. He grabbed me and kissed me. Gently pushing him, I said,

"We need to talk. This is not working out for us. The relationship isn't in a healthy place, and I'm unhappy."

He went on about how much he loves me and wants to please me. He said he would do anything to make it work. He said he would change. He asked me to give him another chance. He refused to let me go until I agreed. Exhausted by his relentless persistence, I agreed and signed away my life on an invisible dotted line. The choice was made, and I was doomed.

Walking away from him, I saw my future waiting to suck the life out of my existence. It was done, and he never returned the money he had borrowed for his flight. I never asked him about it because I didn't know how.

CHAPTER 10

The Professional Emerges

Back in South Africa, after completing my graduate program in Music, I took the plunge and opened my own music business. Teaching at a regular school held no excitement for me. I decided to venture into something entirely different and unique. Both jazz and gospel music were genres not offered by music teachers in Durban. It seemed like a great business idea. Having no knowledge on how to start a business, I identified key business owners and began asking questions. The first step was to come up with a name and then register my new business, Chloe's School of Music.

Once I received approval, I secured a studio space in the heart of the city. It wasn't a difficult find since only one building allowed music lessons due to sound disturbance. Surprisingly, Rob offered to pay the deposit and the first month's rent for the office space as a graduation gift.

With the little money that I had saved, I had to furnish the studio. Enlisting the help of my dad, my brother, Jonathan, and my uncle, Harry, we started brainstorming. Dad and I went shopping for curtain fabric. Uncle Harry and I went shopping for wooden planks to build shelves. Jonathan suggested the most economical way to soundproof the studio, and so we asked everyone we knew to save their cardboard egg cartons. In the Used Furniture section of the newspaper, I found a ridiculously cheap school desk that was badly chipped and scraped. It had to do for the time being, until I could afford something better.

On the first day of business, white curtains with a keyboard printed on it hung by the windows on adjacent walls of the rectangular shaped studio. Dad had sewn them to fit perfectly. He also organized for my piano to be moved from our home to the studio. My Yamaha spinet piano, with its stool neatly tucked in, stood alongside one of the longer walls. Next to it was a simple white plastic chair. That was the seat I would sit on for many hours teaching students how to play the piano. On the opposite side was a cute black school desk. Uncle Harry had worked wonders by sanding it down and giving it a fresh coat of paint. It looked like a designer piece. He could build anything with his hands and had successfully worked in the chips to look like it was intentionally designed. He also made two simple bookshelves from the wooden planks, one in red and one in black. They had a sleek modern look.

Finally, Jonathan covered the common wall between the adjoining offices with cardboard egg cartons. It had the feel and look of a complete studio. After freshening the room with a soft vanilla scent, I was ready to begin my first day of work at Chloe's School of Music. There it was - My very own music studio with my name on the door.

A zero-bank balance! No marketing skills! How on earth was I going to get my business going? I couldn't afford a phone. I couldn't afford to advertise. But I did have my talent, my network, and a fully equipped studio. Based on that, my best strategy was to spread the word. I told everyone; every family member, every friend, and every person I met on the street. I encouraged people to pass the word along. Being a well-known figure in the city was a blessing, so I leveraged my network as the best marketing tool.

In the first month, I recruited only one student. It didn't feel promising! It certainly wasn't the opening I anticipated. Nothing was going to discourage me. Putting my teaching skills to the test with my first student was probably a good thing. This way I could ascertain what worked and what didn't, and then make the necessary adjustments.

Every day for the first month, I showed up faithfully even though I taught just one student for the whole week. Lessons were a half hour long. Before the end of the month, one more student enrolled. It was just enough to pay the next month's rent. I was hopeful and believed I could do anything I put my mind to. I kept saying, *Chloe, you wait and see. It will get better. Students will start enrolling one by one.*

I thought about putting an ad in the paper but didn't have the funds. By the end of the second month, I had four students in total. I got a telephone installed and had enough money left for a newspaper advertisement which appeared every day for the whole week. The first time the phone rang, I almost jumped. My own telephone! And it didn't stop ringing. Things began to take off. It was going to be a success.

Within a year, the total enrollment was up to forty students. It was time to develop a more structured curriculum. The school was becoming popular. I had to turn people away because of limited capacity. Identifying two top talents, Sarah and Lizzie, I proposed an idea to them.

"What if I told the both of you that you could have free piano lessons?"

With a surprised look, they glanced at each other before turning their attention back to me.

"What do we need to do to get free lessons?" Lizzie asked curiously.

"Well, if you're willing to teach Beginner Piano students one day of the week, I'll waive your fees."

"But we won't know where to start," Sarah said.

"That's not going to be a problem. I have a solution."

They listened intently. I could see a sparkle of hope in their eyes.

"If you agree to take me up on the offer, I'll take you through a three-month teachers' training program. At the end of the program, you'll be equipped to teach."

I waited for them to digest the information before I continued. "During the training period, you'll continue paying your fees as usual. At the end of the three months, I'll assign beginner students to you."

They were intrigued. I could tell by the look on their faces.

"One more thing," I added, "If you reach a certain number of students, you'll get paid a percentage of their fees."

Smiles broadened their faces as they stared at me with disbelief. That's when I popped the leading question,

"Why don't the both of you take some time to think about it, and let me know your decision?"

"Do you have any quest…" Before I could finish, the two of them excitedly responded.

"I'm in," Lizzie said.

"So am I," Sarah said. "Thank you for this opportunity."

"When do we start our training?" Lizzie added.

"First, I'll need to design the training program. It will take approximately three months before we can start the training. Are you okay with that?" I asked, wondering if their excitement would dissipate. They eagerly agreed to wait.

After that conversation, I immediately started to expand on the simple curriculum I designed when I opened the studio. Throwing together a few musical concepts, I dove right into ideation mode and began strategizing. What emerged was a newly revised and comprehensive curriculum, divided into three levels of musicality; Beginner, Intermediate and Advanced. Satisfied with the outcome, I began designing an extensive yet simplified teachers' training program. Since both student-teachers would only be focusing on Beginner Piano, there was no immediate need to build out the complete kit. The training covered the syllabi from Grades One through Three. In the meantime, I would continue teaching Intermediate and Advanced Piano.

The phone didn't stop ringing. Instead of turning prospective students away, I decided to start a waitlist. Sarah asked me if she could help at the studio twice a week with administrative duties, and I agreed. While she answered calls, collected fees, and added people to the waitlist, I gave my undivided attention to my piano students, and concentrated on finalizing the training program.

On the days Sarah didn't come in, I had to let the calls go into voicemail. It was overwhelming!

The teachers' training program was complete, and we were ready to go. Registration also got an overhaul with new forms, adjusted fee structures, and revised procedures. It was an exciting time for the Music School. Current students were thrilled with the impending expansion. Both student-teachers anxiously waited for their first teaching experience. Registration for new incoming students was fast approaching, and great anticipation prevailed. It was time to acquire the adjoining studio. I couldn't believe that within two years the Music School had outgrown one studio. We had acquired two studios and two student-teachers. It was definitely a notable milestone for the school.

Over sixty students had enrolled in the new semester. Names still populated the waitlist, and the phone kept ringing. The business surged rapidly contrary to my expectations. It was time to file taxes, which meant I needed an accountant. One of the students recommended Ted, his accountant who was just a few blocks away. I made the call and set up a meeting. After he explained some of the terminologies to me, Ted gave me some tips on bookkeeping and dates to observe. Slowly but surely my business skills were sharpening. If I needed answers, I called Ted or just figured it out on my own. Simply said, I used common sense! An affordable commodity!

Lizzie and Sarah began their first week, nervous and excited at the same time. Both of them came in on separate days since they shared the studio space. After a few months, with the waitlist continually growing, I had a proposition for each of them. The first offer was to Lizzie,

"Listen, Lizzie, I have a proposition for you."

She was all ears as I referred to the growing waitlist. First, I needed to know if she was comfortable taking on more students because my offer was dependent on her answer.

"Lizzie, will you feel comfortable taking on more students?" I asked.

"Yes, Chloe. I would love to."

"What if I offered you a full-time position at the school? I could match your current salary."

Although her eyes lit up, I could detect a moment of caution. After pondering, she said, "Let me think about it."

"That's fine. Take your time. I could offer you a second teaching day, but you currently have a full-time job, and that would present a problem."

"No, I understand," Lizzie replied. I could tell she was trying to process what she had just heard.

The next conversation was with Sarah. I knew she didn't have a full-time job so taking on an extra day would work for her.

"Sarah, as you know, we have a growing waitlist, and I'd like to offer you a second teaching day. Would you be comfortable taking on more students?"

With great excitement, she responded, "Yes, Chloe. I would definitely be comfortable taking on more students. I love teaching. Thank you for considering me."

She had a satisfied look on her face, almost as though she finally understood her calling in life.

"That's great news. So, here's what I'm thinking; for every student you teach above the required number, you'll earn a percentage of their fee. And going forward, you are no longer a student-teacher. You are now a full-fledged teacher."

Sarah was excited. She then went to explain, "Teaching music is my purpose in life, and I'm one hundred percent committed."

A week later, Lizzie accepted the job offer as a full-time teacher. She taught three weekdays and every Saturday. On the two remaining weekdays, while she attended to the administrative tasks including notating lead sheets for songs, Sarah taught in the second studio. The School grew and grew. By the end of our fifth year, we had reached over one hundred twenty students, two full-time teachers, and two new student-teachers, Charmaine and Charlene.

Business was booming. Many students were now at the Advanced level. It was time for Lizzie and Sarah to teach Intermediate Piano. I began building out the Teachers' Training program so they would be equipped to move to the next level. Once they went through the program, they were bumped up to Intermediate Piano, Charmaine and Charlene taught Beginner Piano, and I transitioned out of Intermediate level teaching. I exclusively taught Advanced level. All the teachers and student-teachers were at this level.

I loved watching people enter the studio for the first time, not knowing a single note on the piano. I loved observing them grow and develop into musicians. I loved the sound of music every morning as I walked towards the studio door. I loved the excitement and happiness it brought to the students, the teachers, and myself. I was inspired by every student that journeyed through the school and learned the language of music.

Within a year, they were able to play recognizable tunes fluently. It was transformative; for the student, for the school, for the teacher, and for me! The students couldn't wait to learn their next song. Their repertoire increased week by week, month by month, year by year. They refined their technique with every note on the piano. At the Advanced level, they had the option to specialize in Jazz or Classical music. Most of them opted into the Jazz Program.

At the end of each semester, one week was set aside for piano examinations. External examiners from the University of Kwa-Zulu Natal Music Department and the South African Police Band adjudicated the students who were only allowed to proceed to the next grade if they passed. After a week of examinations, graduation recitals followed. These were cocktail evenings held in conference rooms at the Durban City Hall, where every student got to perform in front of an audience. Prior to the recital, Advanced students were given the opportunity to practice with a band comprising a drummer and bass guitarist to get ready for their performance. It was a magical experience for every musician as they overcame their stage fright, becoming more and more comfortable as performing artists.

Over the years, the Music School attained success and gained nationwide recognition. We had outgrown the space yet again and decided to move the studios to the church premises. There was enough room for multiple teachers as well as access to other instruments. One of the benefits was the availability of the main auditorium for unlimited concert recitals. Before branching off, I decided to change the name of the school to Christian Arts Academy. This was all-encompassing of various art forms. We had expanded and diversified. Satellite schools began to spring up across Durban and the Cape Province. Other instruments were added to the curriculum. Specialists in drums, voice, guitar, bass, and brass instruments were added to the faculty. The Academy had become a household name. My career was established and continued to flourish.

Around the same time, the South African Police Band invited me to sit on their Examining Board. These examinations included candidates from the South African Navy Band as well as the South African Army Band. It was my honor to serve as the civilian examiner. Expanding my network and building on my expertise opened up unexpected possibilities. When the examinations ended, some of the band members approached me and enquired about teaching at the Academy. Recognizing this as an opportunity, I invited them to set up a meeting with me at the Academy to continue the conversation. I didn't want to commit until I had thought it through.

Without realizing it, my business acumen had developed over the years. As a woman, I had become a successful business owner. Not only did I introduce, ignite and develop the gift of music in people, I had also inspired them to find their purpose. The teachers and students loved expressing their music in different forms. Witnessing musicians give birth to their gifts and develop into performing artists fulfilled me. The impact was more significant than I had imagined. Some took up leadership positions at churches, some performed at various venues in the city, and some went on to pursue a degree in music. Every musician used their talent to give back and invest in the lives of people, in the Durban community, and in South Africa our country.

Not a single moment was I alone. Counselor never left me. He guided me and taught me to listen to my heart and the hearts of others. Countless times, students sat at the piano and poured out their hearts. Countless times, I just sat there listening to their stories. Unmeasured tears were shed and innumerable happy moments were shared. The power of music to heal the heart, bring joy to the soul, and breathe life into the artist, is nothing short of phenomenal. Those priceless moments! Unforgettable moments people carried with them for the rest of their lives. The musician may leave the gift, but the gift never leaves the musician. And that's the return on investment with every person who walked through the doors of the Christian Arts Academy.

Every night when I got to bed and closed my eyes, I slipped into the Open Gardens and shared my day with Counselor. Some nights we spent in the Grace Room talking for hours, while other nights we were in the Design Room or the Dark Room. He always had a word of wisdom to share with me. In the Grace Room, I noticed many of the boxes had been opened during the time of the Academy.

"Counselor, I see many of the boxes are opened. And why are there so many opened books left on the table?" I asked.

"Those are the gifts you accessed for the Academy. You didn't know you had all those gifts inside of you. Did you know you were going to be a successful businesswoman?"

"No. I would never have guessed that. If you had told me that before I opened the business, I would have had a hard time believing it," I replied.

Still bewildered, I asked again,

"But why are there opened books lying all around? This place looks like a mess."

Smiling, he uncovered another truth, "Every book holds a chapter of your story. Some chapters have volumes. Those books that you see on the table? That's the story you're living at the moment."

I was overwhelmed by the magnitude held in the Grace Room. He went on,

"When a house is being built, it looks like a big mess. It starts with a design in your imagination. That design is drawn and sketched out in a plan. Then there's contractors and construction. A very messy operation until the finished product. The plan gets filed after the house is complete. That is the same process with life."

In the Design Room lay the multiple pieces of my life. I learned how to weave and stretch, and blend colors and textures. I learned how to translate the lessons into everyday life. And the Dark Room became exciting to visit. The darkness had no power over me. I had no fear because I mastered the skill of self-talk by looking for the light instead of allowing the darkness to overwhelm me. Light represented positivity. I chose to think positive thoughts. And yes, although negative thoughts had an overpowering voice that practically screamed and shouted down positive thoughts, I was adamant. The light was somewhere in the darkness. That's the place I developed as a person, daughter, sister, wife, friend, musician, woman, leader, employer and many other roles.

Opportunities to perform and to lead worship in churches opened for me. Taking on jazz gigs was difficult. Rob would not allow it. My career as a jazz performing artist had come to an end, but I was content passing the gift along to my students. When they performed, I felt I was playing jazz. I experienced their moments with them and through them. That was enough for me. My performing skills had slackened, but I didn't let it get me down. My primary purpose was to pass the gift along to others. What I couldn't have, I made sure others received.

My personal revelation was this: I was living my life and accomplishing my dream through others, since I wasn't able to do or achieve them for myself. I saw the world through their eyes, and I savored the moments as though they were mine. I was happy for everyone who attained satisfaction through their achievements. It felt like I was accomplishing them too. Funny, how my thinking evolved in that way. When it started, I can't tell, but I'm guessing it was from the moment I met Counselor. He coached me on how to survive, and yet still live a full life simultaneously. Sounds impossible, yet very possible. Resilience was my strength and courtesy was my fortitude. Joy came from everything I experienced in life. If I didn't experience it, then I tried my best to find the element of joy in the experience. It happened in the Dark Room. I looked for the light hidden in the darkness.

Without warning, I came face to face with a shadow from my past. During one of my lessons, Charmaine knocked at my studio door and informed me that someone was waiting to see me. He didn't say his name. When the lesson came to an end, I went into her studio, which had a partitioned waiting area. There, sitting and flipping through pages of a music magazine, was George! Not having a rude bone in my body, I smiled and said,

"Hello, George!" How could I greet a man who raped me with a smile? Could I have just been civil without smiling? I seriously didn't know how to. He smiled back and greeted me too. Beckoning him, I invited him into my studio which was adjacent to the second studio. I knew it would be safe because Charmaine entered freely at any time. We had an open-door policy. As soon as I closed the door, he hugged me. I reciprocated not having the space to think and assess my emotions; I was on high alert. His sweet nature was observable, yet I knew differently.

"How are you, Chloe?" he asked.

"I'm doing very well," I responded with some edge of confidence. I realized I had grown and had built up boundaries to safeguard my heart. He just stood there and looked at me for the longest time.

"I have a student waiting so I won't be able to talk," I said.

"What I have to say won't take long," he continued. "First I have never stopped loving you. And secondly, I am sorry for everything that happened. Please forgive me."

"Of course, I forgive you," I said, accepting his apology, which I thought to be reasonably sincere. "It's in the past, and that is over. I've moved on, and so have you." What else could I say? What was the point in holding onto grievances? The past is in the past. I realized nothing I could do or say could change what had occurred. In fact, so many things happened since that horrible day, I had almost forgotten about it.

"I have to say goodbye. My student is waiting and thanks for dropping by. It was good to see you."

As he came to hug me again, the old version of Chloe slipped in. I couldn't say no. I let him. This time, he didn't let go before bending to kiss me. I moved away and said, "You have to leave now. The other teacher will be walking in at any moment."

Just then, Charmaine knocked on the door, opened it and entered. Thank God! We were always so busy that waiting for each other to say, "Come in," didn't really work. Well finally, I felt like I had closure to that part of my life. Relieved it was over; I smiled to myself. I was somewhat proud and empowered knowing I had the willpower to resist his usual sweetness. He had no power over my mind and my emotions anymore.

Being free from George didn't free me from Rob. Rob was my present and possibly my future. I had to find a way to deal with it, but then maybe I had found an unconventional way. Counselor was my North Star. He showed me the path to not just exist, but to live. This was definitely a conversation I had to have with Counselor. Sharing the incident would help me thoroughly process it and put it to rest.

Closing my eyes that night, I found myself in the Design Room. I immediately knew Counselor was going to talk to me about how all the pieces were coming together in some immaculate design. Instead of the shades of white hues, I was accustomed to seeing, splashes of soft colors transformed the design of the room, the hugger chair, the fabrics and textures into something exquisitely unique. It had the illusion of water touching glass. A new design! Right in front of me hung a transparent screen reflecting off the softened colors of the rainbow. It looked magical!

"Walk through the screen, Chloe!" I heard Counselor say.

"Walk through the screen? How?" I asked him.

"Try it and see what happens," he said.

With uncertainty, I decided to explore this screen. Walking toward it, heart racing in anticipation, I knew I was going to discover something beautiful and new. Miraculously, I passed through the screen without even feeling it or touching it.

"How can this be?" I asked Counselor.

"Chloe, you know everything in our world is possible. What exists in your imagination is greater than in real life. Dreams are made in your imagination. Ideas form in your imagination. The future exists in your imagination. The human mind is a mystery to humans. People will continuously discover the power of the mind and never cease to be fascinated by it." He gave me a moment to digest his words and then went on,

"Whenever you develop in the Dark Room and grow accustomed to the light, that revelation is manifested in the Design Room. The more you see beyond the limitations of your mind, the more you realize barriers and boundaries only exist in your mind. Human beings limit themselves to their reality, and that reality is determined by their childhood, their experiences, and the impact of decisions made in life." He waited for me to take it all in, then continued,

"Look around you, Chloe. What do you notice?" As I took in my surroundings, I noticed there was a display of artwork and design from different time periods. It had the look of an art museum. Gazing at the paintings, beautiful furniture and ornaments, I gasped. The paintings reflected my life. I was the object of the artist. The furniture and ornaments were cracked, broken and chipped, yet each crack was the very design that made it beautiful and exquisite. Stunned, I turned to look at Counselor. He was smiling at me.

"Do you remember the old school desk you bought? It was so broken and chipped. It was all you could afford, remember?" Nodding my head to confirm, he then said,

"You thought your uncle Harry worked wonders with it. It looked like a designer piece. That is what happens in this room. Everything in life is redeemable, depending on what you make of it."

Counselor never ceased to amaze me with his wisdom, knowledge, and revelation. He was my inspiration. I wanted to be like him, a counselor. The seed was planted deep in my soul, and the desire burned within me.

"There are screens all around the Design Room. The ones you can't see are your blind spots. Shifting your thinking and opening up your perspective will reveal other screens to you in life. One day when you're ready, you'll invite people to browse through your Design Room. That is how you'll inspire others, by sharing the story of your life."

I will definitely be a counselor one day, I declared to myself. *I'll inspire others to rise from every situation that holds them captive.*

It was time to do something about it. I had shared my gift of music with people. It was time to share my wisdom too.

CHAPTER 11

For Better, For Fear

Reality faced me every time I faced Rob. Certain things were inevitable. The old Chloe still didn't know how to say No; she didn't have the courage to challenge Rob. I could see what my future looked like, but I refused to give into the dismal flashes in my mind. I promised myself I would rise up and make it work. I had to prove to myself, I was a strong woman and could no longer be easily knocked down. I had to convince myself.

Nothing is impossible, Chloe. You can do anything you put your mind to. Just like you built up the business, you can do it in your personal life too.

There was an Indian comedy show playing at one of the theaters in Durban. My dad had purchased tickets for our family to attend. Earlier in the day when I saw Rob, I was too afraid to mention it to him. I knew he would fly off the handle, so I decided not to tell him. That evening, as we were all getting ready to head out to the show, the phone rang. It was Rob. During the call, I was edgy not knowing when he would say goodbye. He wanted to continue talking. I knew I had to find a way to end the conversation. The only way out was telling him the truth. This was his rule; he was the only one who decided when our calls ended. He once said,

"Don't you ever put the phone down before I do. That will make me very angry."

Fear began to rise in my chest, tightening the band around my throat, and causing my breathing to accelerate. I said,

"By the way, I forgot to tell you. Our family is going to see the Indian comedy show everyone is talking about." There was silence on the other end.

My palms were sweaty. Anxiety wrapped itself fiercely around my heart. Feeling like I had just completed a marathon, I spoke in short gasps,

"Are you there?"

Bracing myself for what was to come, I closed my eyes and waited. A tsunami of swear words and derogatory statements gushed out of his mouth. After calling me vile names, he threatened,

"If you step out of the flat tonight, I'll come to the show and make such a scene. You will be embarrassed, and your father will be disgraced. You'll never be able to show your face in the city."

Oh, my God! What kind of monster was I in a relationship with? When will this end? How long would I have to endure this abuse?

"I'm sorry I forgot to tell you. I won't go. I'll stay at home."

Silence. I waited. Nothing.

"Let me go and tell my dad I'm not going," I pleaded, hoping he would say something so we could end the conversation. It would give me a chance to let my parents know.

"I'm calling you in thirty minutes. You'd better pick up the phone," and the line went dead.

"Dad, I don't think I can make it to the show. I have a stomach ache."

"Are you okay? Do you need anything?" my dad asked, believing the lie.

"Don't worry about me. I'll be fine," I said, hiding the sadness behind the deception.

After they left, I cried and cried. Why? Why was I so afraid of Rob? What power did he hold over me? Why couldn't I challenge him? I honestly believed he would kill me if I left him. I really believed it.

Instead of calling thirty minutes later, he called me every ten minutes for the next hour. I was a prisoner behind invisible bars, surrounded by one law enforcement agent who had a paranormal gift to see everything about me without being physically present. Don't ask me how this was possible, but I believed it. If I didn't tell the truth, I thought he would somehow find out. My story seemed like it belonged in a science fiction movie. No one would believe it.

He took it for granted we would get married. He never asked me to marry him. He assumed my answer. This was my rationale. If we got married, then he wouldn't be obsessing about guys making a move on me. We would be together all the time, and I would belong to him. I was sure this would give him peace of mind. I can't count the number of times I wanted to tell him that it was over. I had practiced it so many times.

"Rob, I'm sorry. I don't think you and I are going to work out. We are so dissimilar and value different things in life. I'm not the kind of woman you need. You deserve someone who understands you deeply and can cater to your needs."

But the words never made it out of my mouth. Once I did try to go there, and was shut down to total submission and silence.

"If you don't marry me, I'll tell everyone you're a whore. I'll put an article in the newspapers and disgrace your father."

My God! I was stuck. I could see the end of my life and couldn't wait for it to come sooner than the day I was destined to die. Relinquishing all rights to my life, I knew there was one thing that would always belong to me - my world with Counselor. Rob would never be able to touch that. That was one part of my life where I was entirely in control. I vowed to be wholly committed to my world with Counselor. He always gave me a reason to get up every morning no matter what was going on in real life.

Threatened by Rob, I conceded to marriage. When my parents found out I decided to marry him, they were furious with me. They made it very clear; no one from the family would be attending the wedding. Distressed and crushed, I went ahead and planned my wedding single-handedly. No one was there to help me coordinate it. No one was there to share it with me. Not even a bridal shower was thrown for me. I walked along the road to my future, completely alone. With no way out, I became Rob's wife against my family's wishes.

A few weeks before the wedding, Jonathan sensed my sadness. He said to me,

"Chloe, don't worry! You won't be alone at your wedding. I'll be there to support you."

"But dad and mom explicitly said that the family won't be attending."

"I know what they said. But I'm saying I'll be at your wedding."

I grabbed him and held onto him tightly, in a desperate effort to release the lingering sorrow in my heart. He knew. He wasn't just my brother, he was my best friend.

A few days before the wedding, my mother surprised me.

"Your father and I are not happy that you're marrying Rob. We don't think he is the right person for you. But you are our daughter; so, we've decided to come to your wedding."

What a relief that was for me! My wish was granted!

"Jacob, let's take a look at Chloe's wedding dress and see what we can do to give it our finishing touch."

Dad had a fantastic gift for designing wedding dresses. Over the years, he had sewn numerous gowns while my mother did the most beautiful beadwork and lacework. They were a power team for making so many brides look beautiful on their wedding day. Maybe when she saw the plain wedding dress I brought home, it moved her. No lace. No beads. No pearls. A plain and simple off-the-shoulder neckline wedding dress. One of my close friends owned a florist shop. I had asked her to arrange soft colored flowers of varying lengths, to sew onto my wedding dress on the day of the wedding. It reminded me of my garden with Counselor. It was the only design I wanted for my gown. To please mom and dad, I agreed for them to add two layers of taffeta to give the full floor-length skirt of the gown some flare and volume, and they were right. The gown did need some sprucing up.

I'm not sure at what point my parents changed their minds, but I was glad they did. It meant everything in the world to me. They were disappointed with my choice, but they made every effort to be in the best of spirits, just for me.

This was probably the inspiration behind the Design Room in my heart with multiple textures and shapes in shades of white. The wedding dresses with long trains and veils had to be the source of the Design Room. What an amazing discovery for me! Everything in life somehow fitted together. Counselor was right! It all made sense. Our choices in life come from the resources of our past; the good and the bad. Almost all the time, we are oblivious to this. Our past is a reference point for conscious and unconscious decisions. The night before the wedding, I slept with Ama as she related old tales of love and hope. Then she sang her sweetest lullabies for the last night of my single life to her favorite tune of 'Oh My Darling Clementine.'

That night I dreamed a beautiful dream: The prince from the story Ama told me appeared in my dream. Arrayed in his fine princely robe, he held out his hand to me, with a welcoming kindness in his eyes. It was Counselor. Responding to his open gesture, I placed my hand trustingly in his. I realized I was also dressed in the most exquisite bridal gown fit for a princess. From what I could see, it was gloriously breathtaking and flowing. It reminded me of the textures in the Design Room. He led me onto a crystal dance floor, sweeping me into a smooth fluid waltz. Although I didn't know how to dance and wasn't comfortable on a dance floor, I succumbed to the rhythm and pace of the music. I let him lead me without any inhibitions. Face to face with Counselor, I looked up into his eyes and was taken aback. His eyes reflected my image. I saw myself in his familiar, loving gaze. It was a picture of beauty and grace.

A single string of exquisite pearls hung around my neck. On my crown, sat a petite diamond tiara designed to complement my facial structure framed with delightfully hanging tendrils resting on my nape. Glitter sprinkled all across the exposed parts of my face and neck, giving me an almost ethereal look. Wondering what my shoes looked like, I tore my gaze away from him and glanced at my feet as they continued moving to the three-four beat of the waltz. To my astonishment, they were a pair of glass slippers, just like the ones Cinderella had worn in my fantasy world. I was floating endlessly when the scene changed.

We were gliding on ice. My glass slippers transformed into white ice-skates. My wedding gown transformed into a shimmering dress that ended just above the knees. The sleeveless form-fitted bodice was joined at the waist by flowing leaf-like ribbons. They moved in dramatic fashion with us as we skated in complete synchronicity. This time, Counselor turned me away from him, placed his hands on my waist, then whispered into my ear, "Close your eyes, Chloe. Follow my lead and listen to the rhythm of your heartbeat."

My dream ended there. Maybe I had dreamed what I wished for. Perhaps it was inspired by the fairytales I had read as a child. Maybe Ama's story had triggered an old familiar happiness I experienced as a child before my innocence was invaded. Possibly it was every girl's dream. But for me, Counselor made my dream come true. It was an affirmation of his love for me. I knew then he would always be with me. Somehow, I would find a way to live magnificently. Nothing could keep me down or hold me back. Nothing!

Before the wedding day, forcing myself to be positive, I made my way to the hair stylist and make-up artist. I was sure I would automatically feel cheerful and upbeat. After all, most women feel good walking out of a hair salon or after a facial make-over. It seemed to have the desired effect on me, yet I couldn't put my finger on the range of emotions I was experiencing. Everything was blurred, even my emotions.

On the wedding day, I don't remember getting dressed. I don't remember walking to the elevator in my wedding gown. I don't even remember what the weather was like. But I do remember the conversation on the ride down the elevator as if it was yesterday. Simon had a concerned look of dissatisfaction on his face when he spoke.

"Chloe, this is the moment where you get to change your mind." He studied me for cues whether to proceed or not.

I looked at him blankly at first, not knowing how to respond to his statement.

"Chloe. Why are you marrying him? You realize you're making a big mistake?"

He waited for my answer to his statement that sounded more like a question, but nothing came. Just a small smile. Then he went on,

"You don't have to marry him. It's never too late to change your mind." Again, he waited, but there was silence.

"You don't have to go through with this. Just say the word, and I'll sort everything out." Yet again, I gave him a little smile and said nothing.

"Chloe, you are so talented. You have so many gifts. Think about it. If you marry him, he will never let you reach your full potential. He's not the one for you." And he waited again, prompting me to respond. Nothing came.

"Chloe, you were born to make a difference in the world. Don't do this, Chloe. He'll destroy your life."

I just looked at him and smiled. He was so intuitive. His face. My mom's face. They genuinely cared about my happiness. Both held a look of hopelessness as the elevator made it to the ground floor. The door opened, and I walked toward the future that I had unwillingly accepted, to sign away my true destiny. Every word he said was one-hundred-percent true. He knew. My parents knew. My family members knew. My friends knew. Everybody knew, and no one could do anything about it. The big difference was this: They knew half the story, while I knew the whole story. I said nothing, just responded silently to myself;

If only you knew Simon, if only you knew.

It was a small, sad wedding. In total, forty close friends and family attended from both sides. My family members didn't dress up like one would dress up for a wedding. There was no excitement in the air. People smiled and congratulated us, but their smiles didn't reach their eyes. Through it all, I pretended, smiled and chose to bring my heart to the nuptials. It was over.

That first night as a married woman lacked romance, anticipation, and fulfillment. It was awkward and void of true love. There was nothing to write about.

Two days later, we left for our honeymoon to London and Europe. The thought of an adventure excited me. Our plan was to stay with my uncle Will in London for one whole week, then travel on to other European countries using the 21-day Eurail pass. The thrill of the unknown awaited us. Rob liked playing and living dangerously. Although I loved the thrill of the unknown, danger wasn't a game I played. I enjoyed breaking certain rules, but was discerning as to how far I could push the limits, while still adhering to the law and exploring possibilities.

On our way to London, we had a layover in Luxemburg in the early parts of the morning. All passengers were required to go through Passport Control even though we were in transit. Standing in line behind Rob, I must have turned away from him for a few seconds when he disappeared. Anxiously I scanned the crowds. He was nowhere to be seen. This couldn't be happening. Where was he? My heart pounded viciously against my ribcage. Suddenly, I was afraid. Standing on tiptoes to look over the crowds to where the immigration officer sat, I saw Rob on the other side, waving his hands to get my attention. How did he get past the immigration officer?

I motioned to him to inquire how he got there so quickly. He signaled for me to take a route to bypass immigration. Oh, my God! I couldn't believe what he did. The immigration officer was stamping everyone's passport which meant they would be rechecking it before we boarded the plane. How would he account for his entry into Luxemburg without a stamp on his passport? What a sneaky man! Unafraid of people in authority and always challenging house rules like it was a game, he played dangerously. It frightened me. He continued beckoning me, but I shook my head in disagreement. All I could think was about Rob getting caught. How embarrassing it was going to be for me! There was no way he would be able to get back in line. What if the immigration officer thought I was his accomplice in some weird scheme? It started to look bad. As the bleak consequences of his actions took multiple turns and directions in my head, another shock hit me.

He was standing next to me. How was that possible? I couldn't believe his gall. This is what con artists do. Shocked, disgusted and disappointed at the same time, I asked him,

"How did you get back on this side?" Impatiently waiting to hear his response, he casually replied,

"When the immigration officers weren't looking, I slipped right past them. They didn't even notice me." He said it with a sense of pride and accomplishment.

What on earth went on in his mind? Why was such a thing thrilling for him? I just couldn't understand. I was married to a shrewd conniving man. Unashamedly, he made an outrageous offer as he pulled my hand,

"Come with me. Let's go. Just follow me. We won't get caught."

What extent would this man go to, I thought. I pulled my hand away from his and said, "No."

"Let's go," he persisted. "We won't get caught. Trust me."

There was no way I could trust him. At that moment, he lived above the law. I couldn't go along with him because I abided by the law.

"No. I'm not going with you. I don't want to get caught."

Fed up with my response, he unwillingly surrendered and stood in line with me, complaining all the way about how scared and unadventurous I was. I didn't want to think about what I would be coming up against for the rest of the trip. But my back was up against the wall. I was on my guard. I didn't want to be thrown in jail in some foreign country. Rob was a worldly man; too worldly for me.

It was a dull greyish day when we arrived in London. Uncle Will was waiting for us at Heathrow Airport. It was wonderful seeing him after so many years. Exhausted from the unexpected adventures and the jetlag, we showered, ate dinner prepared by Uncle Will, and then went straight to bed. We probably slept for almost twelve hours, the first full night's rest since the wedding.

Tomorrow would be the first regular day of our honeymoon and the rest of our lives as husband and wife. God help me!

When we got up, it was dark outside. Feeling disoriented with no sense of time, I asked Uncle Will,

"Is it evening already? We must have slept for a very long time." Smiling in his cool tender way, he answered with a question,

"What time do you think it is, Chloe?"

"7 p.m. or 8 p.m.," I replied. He threw back his head and laughed.

"It is 10 a.m."

"Then why is it so dark outside?" I asked.

"This is London, Chloe." Surprised, all I could respond with was, "Wow!"

After breakfast, he gave up some tips on how to get around in London, where to go, and what to see. It was freezing, and I was all togged up, but Rob was dressed lightly. When Uncle Will saw what he was wearing, he asked,

"Rob, are you going to put on a warm coat, and a scarf and hat?"

"No. I'll be fine," Rob replied.

"It's freezing out there. You'll catch a cold."

Rob was insistent. As far as he was concerned, he had control over everything, even the weather. So off we went to explore London. I had made up my mind to enjoy myself regardless of Rob's display of arrogance. Making the best of any situation came from years of practice. London was nothing short of spectacular, even in the freezing cold. I loved every moment of it, even the lengthy conversations with Uncle Will, hearing him retell the adventures of his life after he left South Africa. It was nostalgic bonding with him, and getting to know him more intimately. By the end of the week, I was sad to be leaving London and Uncle Will. Rob, on the other hand, had the sniffles. I hoped it was only the sniffles.

Our first stop was in Paris. It was beautiful; everything I had dreamed it would be. Rob started to slow down because he now had a full blown cold. We still had twenty days left on the Eurail pass. We planned to travel to the farthest city at night while we slept in our first-class cabin, showered at the train station, left our bags in the station lockers, and explored the city during the day. The next stop was Venice, the city of romance and love. I somehow compartmentalized what was going on with Rob and my exploration of these European cities. Being able to shut off negativism, while being bombarded by it, was a gift. Survival was key. I couldn't let him bring me down with his attitude, which was pretty pathetic by then. Granted, he wasn't feeling well, so I didn't expect him to be vibrant and alive. But I blamed him for his condition, even though I wouldn't dare say anything.

When we arrived in Venice, he told me he couldn't make another long journey on the train. We needed to check into a hotel for the night. After finding affordable lodgings, I wanted to explore Venice. Upset that I would even consider enjoying myself while he was sick, he resorted to the silent treatment. What a honeymoon! At that moment, I knew without a shadow of doubt I had made the worst decision of my life; I married the wrong man. Again, I compartmentalized, and made my way around Venice, discovering the gorgeous waterways by gondola. It was euphoric! Not a single moment was I alone. Counselor was with me. Everywhere I went, in the midst of crowds, I always took a moment to ponder and share my experiences with Counselor. Bystanders couldn't see what was going on in my world. All they saw was a young woman gazing at the glorious Venetian sights. I guess they probably didn't even notice I was there.

The next day, we checked out of the hotel and made our way to Nice. Rob was really sick. He had layers of clothing and continuously coughed up mucus. If he could afford to stay at the hotel for the rest of the time, he would have. He had no option, but to keep moving. I knew he needed a doctor, medication, and rest. When we got to Nice, I suggested we check into a cheap hotel and look for a doctor, which he agreed to.

"You need to see a doctor. If you can't afford it, then put the charges on your credit card,"

"Ask someone at the reception for a list of the doctors close by," he said.

Nodding, I made my way downstairs to make inquiries. Thank God there was a doctor right around the corner. No one could speak English well, not even the doctor, but we took our chances. The diagnosis was pneumonia. Rob had the symptoms. I had signs we were never meant to be together, but I remembered what Counselor once said,

"Everything that happens doesn't always happen for a reason, but you can find a reason in it. Some things may not make sense, but all things have a place in your purpose."

His finances were something we never discussed. I didn't know what he earned or what he had in his bank account. That was a taboo topic! With my finances, it was full disclosure. I didn't know better since this was my first proper relationship with a man. When he said, he didn't have the money, I believed him. How he paid the doctor and the extra night at the hotel, I have no idea. He made sure I wasn't around when he paid both bills.

We stayed in Nice for two days. After the doctor's visit, Rob slept for the rest of the day with the curtains drawn. He didn't want any light in the room. Feeling sympathetic towards him, I sacrificed sightseeing and decided to stay indoors in the dark for the rest of the day. I had to stop myself from blaming him for his condition.

"He brought this upon himself," I thought, but never out loud.

The day was long and tedious with nothing to do. I took out my travel log and began journaling, being extra careful as to what I wrote, scrutinizing every word and every sentence that could be misconstrued. I realized the woman Rob was married to was someone else; it was his version of a wife. He never knew me. The real Chloe existed in my dream world; a place where incredible things happened. Counselor was there. I was there, and intruders could never get passed the iron-clad lock; they didn't have my heartbeat. My secret thought life was way out of Rob's control. If he knew what was going on inside my mind, I figured he would kill me. I could never let him in, nor anyone else for that matter. People would think I was crazy. My secret was safe with Counselor and me.

I never believed that one day I would be writing my memoirs and sharing my vulnerabilities with the world. If Counselor had said to me that someday I would be an author writing a story about the real Chloe, I wouldn't have believed him. Another gift from the Grace Room.

The second day in Nice, Rob felt a little better and decided to do some sightseeing with me. Still feeling weak, he opted for an escorted tour. That way he didn't have to walk all the time. Everything in Nice looked like a painting. It was beautiful. Mediterranean beaches, Art Deco architecture, a stunning palace with an impressive display of musical instruments, romantic gardens, alluring fountains, and streets with picturesque cafes. A romantic spot for lovers! But not for us.

By the end of our trip, Rob was back to his old self, but the honeymoon was over. We did have some wonderful moments when I chose to shut out the not-so-pleasant incidents. My choices determined the experience I wanted to have, so I chose wisely. Honeymoons are supposed to be a romantic vacation where happy memories are created. I wondered if our honeymoon was a precursor to what our married life was going to be like. I hoped I was wrong.

CHAPTER 12
A Mattress of Roses and Thorns

Being back home in South Africa, with the wedding and the honeymoon behind us, we settled down to start our lives together. Was the honeymoon an accurate indicator of what our married life was going to be like? I had to wait and see.

A few months before getting married, we purchased a small two-bedroom ranch style house on a quarter acre land, filled with tall trees and bushes in a secluded area. It was about fifteen minutes away from the city center. Besides the few months I spent in Rochester, I had never really lived away from my parents or understood the responsibilities of owning a house. Growing up in a block of flats in the heart of the city was the only lifestyle I knew. Forced to take Rob's lead on almost everything, I agreed to contribute fifty percent to our living expenses, which I thought was fair.

Furnishing the house was pretty cheap, since Rob got most of the pieces at a ridiculously reduced price from the store where he worked. He used part of his savings to get us started, since he was much better off financially. He was established way before I opened the Academy.

Adjusting to married life and a new house wasn't easy. I was always afraid, especially when I was home alone, thinking about who or what was lurking in the darkness of the trees and bushes. It was unfamiliar territory for me. The newspapers ran daily reports on house break-ins and car hijackings. I certainly didn't feel safe. Although we had an alarm system, I couldn't sleep at night. Every small sound echoed in the dark, and almost every night I got Rob up to investigate.

"Rob! Get up!" I whispered, "I can hear noises outside."

Getting up, he would listen intently, but there was nothing. He didn't know whether to believe me or not. I was becoming paranoid, and I couldn't talk myself out of it.

In addition to my increasing fears, Rob limited visits to my parents. We only had one car plus I didn't have a driving license yet. I was twenty-eight years of age. That was primarily due to the Indian culture: Men did most of the driving. Usually, women who were more independent got their license. I was entirely at Rob's mercy; visiting my dad and mom whenever he decided to take me. Fear was quickly becoming my foe. I felt walls closing in on me from all sides; it was thick, grey and gloomy. My connection to Counselor was weakening. Fear rose up as a barrier between him and me. I prayed daily that God would make a way for us to move out of the house.

Trapped with no place to run or hide, I continually sensed the impending danger. There had to be a way to escape. Rob perceived my fears. He could see it in my eyes. Ironically, he became the lesser fear compared to what lurked outside.

On Mondays, I didn't go into the office. It was my day off. Every door and every window remained shut until Rob came home. The television was blasted to drown out any noise from the outside. Rob began to realize my fears were real so he suggested getting a dog. That was another problem. Growing up in the flat, we had an adorable toy Pomeranian, Neil. I was definitely not used to big dogs, but I decided to go along with his suggestion. On the weekend, we visited the SPCA and found a cute six-month-old black Labrador, Dexter. When we got home, he jumped around playfully, causing me to lose my balance since I was small in stature. It wasn't a good sign because I didn't have the tenacity to make any more adjustments. Dexter wanted me to play with him, but I didn't know how, especially with all his excitable jumping. He definitely didn't make it easy.

It took a few weeks for him to settle in. After the first ten minutes of jumping, he calmed down and turned into a docile lovable dog, comfortably resting his head on my lap. He was really adorable. Dexter was friendly with everyone, which didn't help because we needed a watchdog.

While he began to grow on me, my fears remained the same. Instead of relaxation, Mondays were becoming a dread. It was a Sunday evening when I said to Rob,

"Tomorrow, please drop me off at my parents' home. I can't stay here alone. I'm too afraid."

"Okay, I'll drop you off," he agreed even though he didn't like the idea.

What a relief! As soon as I got to my parents' place, I felt such a sense of peace for two reasons: I was finally going to relax, and I got to spend time with my mom. It was going to be a great day until the phone rang about two hours later. It was Rob.

"The alarm company called to say someone tried to break into the house." Instinctively, I stiffened. The fear brewing inside of me rose up like a raging volcano.

"What did they say?" I asked, with a tone of urgency, afraid to hear the answer.

"They broke the large window in the bedroom," was all I heard him say.

The only room with a large window was our bedroom. If I were home, I would have been laying on the bed.

"What?" I practically screamed. Rob was quiet on the other side. He knew this was a point of no return for me.

"We have to sell the house. I refuse to live there anymore. I can't live there. I'm too afraid." I pleaded with desperation. Rob had to agree.

"It's not something we can do overnight," he said. "It will take a few months. We can talk to a few agents and see who gives us the best appraisal."

Thank God! He answered my prayers. This would also mean I got to spend Mondays with my parents. Rob wasn't too happy with that, but he didn't have an option. He always wanted me for himself.

One evening when we got home, Dexter was missing. We drove around the neighborhood looking for him. He was nowhere to be found. We weren't too surprised because he was always running away, but this time he never came back home. We waited for a week before deciding to go to the SPCA and get another dog. That's when Bentley, a cross between a German Shepherd and a Rhodesian ridgeback, and his mom, Belle, a true Rhodesian ridgeback, made their way into our lives and into our hearts. I fell in love with the both of them. They made me feel safe, especially Belle, who was a fantastic watchdog. Nothing and no one got past her. No one was allowed to even touch me! She was my guardian angel.

To get a good appraisal and make a profit on the sale of the house, renovations had to be done before we put it on the market. Uncle Harry offered to help. He had an eye for design. He could take anything not worth looking at, and transform it into something beautiful, just like he did with the desk for my office. After sharing his ideas, he got to work, transforming my simple house into a quaint delightful home.

Sadly, I would have to leave his handiwork for the next owner to enjoy. While he stayed with me, I was brave because I didn't have to be alone in the house. He was like my second dad. He didn't have a family of his own, nor did he have children. I could tell him almost anything. He was a real cool dude! I loved him with all my heart. And so, we sold the house at a profit after living there for just under a year.

I wanted to live closer to the city in a well-developed area with houses, condos, malls, shops, and people in the vicinity. We found a pristine Edwardian three-bedroom cottage, light blue in color with white details. Inside were gorgeous high ceilings, beautiful hardwood floors, wood carvings and trimmings, and stained glass windows. Behind the house was a well-kept small garden with only one tree. That was totally manageable for me. Finally, I was free from the fear of the tall trees and bushes in the secluded areas.

Now that we settled into a somewhat regular rhythm in the new house, Rob defaulted to his old selfish patterns again. He had full access to my finances and controlled my visits to my parents. In front of people, he was on his best game. Being an extrovert, he took over the conversations with his flamboyant mannerisms and worldly experiences. I usually listened, and if I had something to say, he openly shut me down in public. To avoid embarrassment, I had to be discerning; know when to speak and when to refrain from speaking.

Most of our friends were my friends from church. At first, he was insistent on me joining his church, but I couldn't do that. I was too involved as the Music Director in my church. Rob, on the other hand, wasn't involved in any church activities. There was no way I could leave the support structure I had formed with friends from my Christian community. He gave in once he got to know my friends.

On Tuesday evenings, we attended an hour-long prayer meeting at the church. Every week after work, on our way to the meeting, we dropped in at my parents' place for dinner. This was very convenient for Rob. Firstly, we had to eat something. Secondly, we got to spend time with my parents, but most of all, it was limited time; only an hour-and-a-half every week. Things worked out perfectly for him. Jonathan who still lived with my parents was always asking Rob to come by. Those visits were too few and far in-between. As long as I played by Rob's rules, everything was okay.

We usually visited Rob's parents' home every two weeks. As soon as we entered their house, Rob was treated like a king. His mother made sure he had everything he wanted. If she didn't wait on him, then she made sure his father did. She adored her son. Sometimes we visited on a weekday after work. When Rob entered the house, he headed straight for the recliner. Before sitting, he kicked off his shoes, took off his work pants, shirt and tie. His mother would then hurry to get him a pair of shorts, tee-shirt and sandals. Some of his clothes were still at his parents' home. He demanded, and they delivered.

One day I asked Rob to get me a glass of water because I was too shy to wander into the kitchen. Immediately, his mother interjected and told me to get it myself. She said, "You should be seeing to him. Not the other way around."

Out of respect, I didn't comment. I just sat there. Rob knew I was uncomfortable, so he got up and brought me a glass of water. When it came to his family, his opinions were held in the highest regard. Watching these scenes and listening to those types of conversations always bothered me, but I didn't want to come between Rob and his mother. I felt it was none of my business. With all her loving gestures, he shouted at her and spoke disrespectfully. Not once did I hear him have a father-son conversation with his dad. He was always shouting him down. It disturbed me that he would treat them with such disrespect, and I thought to myself, *Then who am I? Why would he treat me any better?*

He respected no one. He didn't take directions from people. He only gave directions. Once he tried to talk back to my dad, but couldn't get away with it. My dad immediately put him in check.

Around this time, South Africa was in an upheaval. Things were coming to a head in the political arena with Nelson Mandela's impending release from prison. Uncertainty swept through the whole nation. Not knowing in which direction the winds would blow, non-white people took their stance. It was our time to stand for freedom and to link arms in the fight for equality.

Realizing the time had come for a call to action, I decided to gather musicians and singers in the city of Durban, and to sound the final battle cry in a celebratory concert. Pulling together many performing artists to unite in solidarity, I convinced them to be part of this notable event in the history of our country.

Excitement ignited the city as the build-up to Mandela's release was fast approaching. Collaborating with Sipho Namba, a famous artist during that time, we composed *The Peace Song* as the finale for the Freedom Concert leading up to the first South African democratic elections. Freedom was so close, we could taste it in the air, and sense it was vibrating in our souls.

The concert was scheduled to be held at the church I attended. Discussing the plan with the pastors of the church wasn't an easy conversation. It wasn't well received. They refused to be involved because they firmly believed there would be bloodshed in the streets and people wouldn't come to the concert.

With my faith in greater things to come, I marched forward relentlessly. Singers came from all over the city, totaling about one hundred outstanding voices. The top talent pool of musicians was excited to be part of this historical moment. Feeling confident that success would follow, I called news reporters, people from the media, and passed the word along to as many influential people I was connected to: "We're coordinating a concert in celebration of freedom and peace. All the top musicians and singers in the city of Durban will be joining forces, and be performing on stage together, in anticipation of a new democratic South Africa."

That night, the auditorium was packed to capacity. People came from far and wide. The media was there broadcasting live. Cameras were flashing. Interviews were taking place. People were starting to believe the impossible was possible. A spirit of celebration spread across the audience of all colors; Blacks, Whites, Indians, Coloreds. As the choir lifted over one hundred voices in skillful African harmony singing 'The Peace Song,' the message resounded in the very souls of all who were oppressed, and of those who observed the oppressed but were powerless to do anything. It was the dawning of a new day for South Africans. Every person would have a voice. No longer would there be a supreme race. All citizens would share in the glory of this democracy. It was a night to remember in the history of South Africa. It was my honor to be part of this great shifting in the political climate. The world was watching, and we were on the brink of a new South Africa. What a remarkable occasion! Those were the days we hold forever as precious memories. As Mandela walked the long walk to freedom, we walked with him singing,

"Nkosi Sikelel' iAfrika!" translated "God Bless Africa."

After two years of marriage, it was time to think about having a baby. Rob had a seven-year-old son from his previous marriage who stayed with us every two weeks. It was always a pleasure having him around. He brought out the child inside of me, and I made every effort to make him happy. If I was going to have a baby of my own, then the first thing I needed to get was my drivers' license.

In the meantime, Simon had just purchased a new car and wanted to sell his gold BMW 3 Series. Jonathan suggested I buy it from him,

"Chloe, Simon is selling his BMW. You should think about purchasing it from him, It's really charming and just the right size for you. That way you can have some independence. You can't be so dependent on Rob all the time. The more you rely on him, the more you'll forget who you are. You need to start standing on your own two feet."

"I know, Jonathan, but you know how he is. He'll never let me drive on my own. I can't see it happening."

"Well, you got to have faith. Talk to him about it and see what he says."

Jonathan was right. Getting my license, owning a car and being able to drive it, would definitely give me some independence. Obviously, the transition wouldn't be easy, but it was worth a try. That evening I needed to have a conversation with Rob about it.

"Jonathan called today and told me that Simon is selling his BMW," I said as a matter of fact.

"Is he buying a new car?" Rob asked.

"Yes, that's what Jonathan said. You know, it got me thinking. If we're planning on having a child, I would need to get my drivers' license. His car would be a great starter car for me. It's cute, and it's in excellent condition. What do you think?"

"I think it's a good idea. How much is he selling it for?" Entirely taken aback, I didn't want to show my surprise at his response,

"I don't know. I didn't ask," even though I already knew the price.

I didn't know if he was testing me. I had to play him at his own game. Was Rob finally feeling secure in our marriage, I wondered? This was a huge step for him. As casually as possible, I said,

"I'll ask him when we talk again,"

"If you can afford it, then buy it. Maybe Simon will reduce the price for you."

"Okay. I'll talk to him," I said, bringing the conversation to a close, not wanting to linger or sound too enthusiastic.

Nodding his head in agreement meant everything to me. I didn't want him to know how happy I was, in case he changed his mind. I learned how to mask my emotions. I couldn't be too happy, nor too upset. Finding a balance between how much and how far was a well-practiced skill. Although I lived a pretend life with Rob and with the rest of the world, my real life was with Counselor. He taught me how to live a balanced life. It wasn't always easy, but I certainly tried. And now, I had Bentley and Belle, my two faithful best friends.

A few months later, after a check-up, I got a call from the doctor's office to say I was six weeks pregnant. Since my cycle was never regular, I had no idea. Immediately, I called my parents and told them the good news. They were happy for me. It would be their first grandchild. My second call was to Rob's mother. Instead of receiving the same enthusiasm, she was upset.

"You think we don't know you're pregnant? Everyone knows you're about three months pregnant, and you're only telling us now."

I was so confused. Where did she get that information from? No one knew besides my parents who I just got off the phone with. Rob's mother refused to believe me. I tried to tell her she was misinformed, but she was adamant. Then I said,

"Well let's wait and see when the baby arrives. Time will tell," and I left it there.

I didn't allow that moment to take away my joy or dampen my celebration. That evening, Rob bought me roses to celebrate and took me to visit my parents. My side of the family celebrated with us. Rob didn't understand why his mother would think that way. If he had any conversation with her regarding the misunderstanding, I never knew about it. He didn't relate his conversations with his mother to me, and I understood as this was a relationship between a mother and her son.

The second piece of good news: I was a proud owner of a car. I eventually bought the car from Simon. To me, it was a great accomplishment. In the meantime, I brushed up on my driving skills to take the test. Without my permission, Rob began using my car to work. I didn't mind, since I needed to get my license. Rob started work at 7 a.m., while I only needed to be at my office by 10 a.m. He usually sent a driver from his job to pick me up from home and drop me off at work. I was three months pregnant when I took my driving test and passed. Smiling to myself I thought, "My baby took the test with me."

The next morning, thinking I was going to drive my car to work, I was apprehensive. Rob got up in the morning as usual and took my car. The driver came to pick me as usual. The same thing happened the next day, and the next. And, I didn't know how to tell him I wanted my car back. Whenever he spoke about the BMW, he referred to it as his car. Anger began to rise inside of me. I knew he had some devious plan; he wanted me to pay for the car while he drove it. I felt like he had conned me into buying the car for him.

Too scared to confront him, I said nothing, as usual. Jonathan, who was incredibly intuitive, especially about things concerning me, asked me,

"Why aren't you driving the car now that you have your license?" Being honest with him, I said,

"Because he just took the car and he isn't giving it back to me."

"Well, did you say anything to him?"

"No, Jonathan. You know I can't say anything. I just have to let it be."

Jonathan shook his head and commented,

"If you don't say something, things will never change, and you'll always live like this." I knew he was right, but I couldn't complain to Rob. I played it safe for the sake of my marriage. There was no way I could upset the cart, so I let it be. Rob's old Mercedes sat in the garage.

One day, his dad who worked late hours, called him to say his car had broken down. In my sleep, I could hear Rob tell him to get someone to drop him off at our house. It was after midnight when the doorbell rang. I thought Rob was going to give him a ride home. Instead, he gave him the keys to his old Mercedes. Now I was wide awake with my eyes tightly shut. Scenarios began to play in my mind. I knew for a fact his dad was a reckless driver and was always knocking up his car. When we got up in the morning, I was revved,

"When will you get your car back because I need to start driving my car?"

The words finally made it out of my mouth. And since it was out, I didn't hold back.

"He'll return it when he gets his car fixed," he said sheepishly.

"And when will that be?" I pushed.

Rob was now getting angry and turned it on me like he always did.

"Would you stop overreacting? You're making something out of nothing" and he walked away.

He has a knack for making me feel like everything was always my fault or I was being too emotional. The fact is, his father never returned Rob's car and didn't ever fix his car again. Every time I brought up the subject, Rob would say,

"I'm not going to ask him for the car."

So, my car became his car. There were so many things he sneakily made me pay for, like the plane fare to New York City when I was still a student. Another time was the timeshare. I wanted to invest in a timeshare with Resorts Condominium International (RCI). The both of us went to the Sales Office down the road from our home to inquire about a timeshare. At the end of the conversation, I paid for the timeshare with my credit card, but somehow the membership reflected his name. Again, he did things underhandedly. He was smooth, slick and sneaky. Even though I was a perceptive woman, when it came to Rob, I still couldn't tell when he was conning me. I fell for it every time, and it was always too late.

When the RCI membership card arrived with his name on it, I didn't have the guts to ask him why. I was afraid, so I let it slide, but in my heart, I held a grievance. He couldn't tell because I was good at it, just like he was good at conning. The both of us were masters in our own field.

The physical intimacy we shared, lacked love and tenderness. Every time we made love, I felt dirty. I didn't know what was good and what was bad. All I knew was what he showed me and told me. He was my only point of reference, so I had to believe him. I longed to feel loved and valued. I longed to be treated like a precious jewel. I longed to feel like a princess. I longed to know what it felt like to be a woman who is loved. This was my bed. This was the mattress I lay on every night. It had roses, and it had thorns. I often thought to myself, *Maybe this is what married life is supposed to be like.*

I convinced myself there was nothing more to it. Maybe my expectations were too high or unrealistic. After all, I was a big daydreamer. I lived in a secret world with Counselor. That's when I slipped into my dream world.

I lay on a soft bed of rose petals with the divine scent of sweetness brushing over me tenderly. With my eyes closed, I knew exactly where I was; in the Rose Garden by the Healing Baths. I turned my body, so the side of my face rested against the silkiness of the petals, and with the rest of my body partially facing the rose bed. With open palms, I slowly ran my hands against its softness. I didn't want to open my eyes for I could see everything with my eyes closed. So, this is the inspiration for the Rose Garden; my mattress of roses and thorns. The only difference was that Counselor had removed all the thorns.

"You've been removing the thorns on your own Chloe," he said.

Opening my eyes, I saw him sitting on a bench looking at me, wondering what he meant.

"I don't remember removing the thorns. When did I do that?"

"You do it every day when the going gets tough. You've been doing it for so long that it's now second nature to you. Whenever you find a way to survive or bounce back or heal, you're removing the thorns. The amazing thing is that you always find a way."

Counselor was right. I do find ways to live my life no matter what goes on. Sometimes it is very challenging. There are times when it's hard to bear, but I somehow make it through the forest.

"Today I'm going to take you to a part of the garden you've never visited before. I gave you a glimpse of it in real life. When you see it, you will know."

Counselor had my full attention. *I wonder what it could be,* I thought.

"Come with me," he motioned towards the back of the garden.

As we walked in silence along the narrow winding pathway, there was a slight incline. The smell of wet grass and foliage was refreshing. Stopping for a few moments, I lifted my face toward the sun, closed my eyes and allowed its warmth to touch my skin. Stretching out both hands, I took a deep breath of the crisp, fresh air. It was so peaceful. When we reached the end of the garden, there was a hedge along the back length. I wasn't sure what Counselor wanted me to see. The only thing he didn't show me was the fourth room in the Big Red Heart. Every time I thought about asking him, something else always had my attention. I wondered if this had something to do with the fourth room. I didn't even know what it was called.

"So now what happens?" I asked Counselor, as we both stood and faced a thick high green hedge.

"Close your eyes," he said. Intrigued, I willingly obeyed. Then he went on,

"Now, imagine what lays behind this hedge. Allow your imagination to take you beyond this point. Remember I'm right here with you. Let it go wherever it wants to go. Don't hold back! I'm standing next to you." He touched my arm to reassure me.

"This is like the time we were in the Dark Room. There, I didn't need to close my eyes because everything was dark."

He didn't say anything, which made me think he wanted me to explore freely. Like the speed of a comet flying through the air, I was transported deep into a dark forest. Suddenly, I couldn't breathe. It was the tall trees and bushes of the dark secluded area of our first house. On the verge of dragging myself from the image, Counselor quickly placed his arm loosely around my shoulders.

"Don't be afraid! Just stay with it for a little while longer. I'm here with you."

Trusting Counselor, I forced myself to let my imagination roam freely. Once I began to adjust to the darkness around me, I realized my breathing was slowing down.

"Now open your eyes," he said. With deliberation, I opened my eyes cautiously. I was in a thick forest.

"How did we get here?" I asked Counselor.

"Your imagination is a powerful tool. It can take you anywhere you want it to, in and out of danger, and in and out of fear. You see, fear exists in your mind only. Look around you! Because it's dark, it doesn't mean it's dangerous."

"That's true! The whole thing was in my mind. I couldn't see you because I only saw my fear. You've told me that before."

"Look around you! What do you see? What can you hear? What do you feel? What can you smell?"

As I looked and beheld the beauty of the forest, I realized this was all part of my garden. It smelled fresh and inviting. The air was clean and crisp. The coolness of the forest lay against my skin, rejuvenating every cell in my body. I could hear the chirping of birds and the unusual sounds belonging to this exotic place. Looking up, I saw birds in a variety of colors flying graciously from treetop to treetop. But best of all was the last thing I noticed. Still looking up, there was the dazzling sun peering into the forest. As she threw her rays across the high branches, it appeared like the splendor of heaven touched this beautiful scene with triumph and wonder. Nothing could be hidden in its brilliance.

I knew why he brought me here without even asking him. He wanted me to get over my fears. Counselor left no stone unturned. A glorious experience! The grandeur of the tall trees and bushes in the dark secluded places held a compelling mystery and wonder for me.

It was the second week of September. My baby was due in two weeks. The nursery was ready, and my hospital bag was packed. I was really excited and oblivious to the endless schemes of Rob. I was focused on my baby. Around midnight, the phone rang. Rob answered. It was his dad. Immediately, I became anxious.

"Now, what could it be?" I wondered.

Rob was silent on our end. Pretending to be asleep, I was curious about what his father was saying. I heard Rob say,

"Well, can you get someone to drop you off at my house?"

After Rob put the phone down, I got up and asked him, "What happened to your father?"

"He said the car wouldn't start, so he needs a ride home."

Just as I thought. I knew this day would come. Fed up, I turned and went back to sleep.

About twenty minutes later, the doorbell rang. Rob got up. I heard voices outside, but I didn't care to listen to what was being said. About ten minutes later, Rob locked the front door and jumped back into bed. There was no way the thought running through my mind could be true. No way!

"How is your father going home?" I asked.

"I gave him the BMW," was all I heard. I was livid and almost hysterical.

"How can you give your father my car without my permission?" Without any feeling of guilt or regret he said,

"Stop overreacting! He's going to drop it off in the morning on the way to church."

"But that's my car! Why didn't you ask me?" By now I was screaming. Rob met my screaming with his own raised voice.

"Don't you scream at me!"

"I'm sure your car already had knocks because your father handles things recklessly. Your mother is always telling you that," I retorted.

He turned his back to me, switched off the light, and fell asleep. Of course, I cried the whole night. I didn't get to drive my own car.

Early the next morning, the phone rang. Rob answered. It was his mother. I could hear some commotion, but didn't want to make any assumptions. However, I had a queasy feeling in the pit of my stomach. After putting the phone down, he said,

"My dad broke the gear stick so he can't drive the car. We'll have to get a mechanic to fix it."

Another argument broke out. He knew I had had it. This was the final straw for me. He called Jonathan and asked him to pick us up for church. When Jonathan came by, he just looked at me, and his eye spoke volumes. Rob and I didn't speak on the way to church. After service, we usually went out for lunch with some of the young couples. During lunch, I tried to ask him,

"What are you going to do about the car? Who's going to fix it?" He shouted me down in front of everyone. Being two weeks away from giving birth, I could feel anxiety overtake me. My head was spinning. My chest was tight. When Jonathan dropped us off, Rob and I were not speaking to each other. The biggest irony of all was that in his twisted mind this had become my fault again.

I had a sharp pain in my abdomen. When I went to the restroom, I was spotting. Too afraid to say anything, I knew I needed to calm down and rest. I slept for the rest of the afternoon. Taking it easy on Monday and Tuesday, I listened to Bach's *Brandenburg Concertos* and Mozart's *Eine Kleine Nachtmusik* to keep my mind healthy and stress free. Early Wednesday morning, the pains returned and intensified. Thank God, Rob got someone to fix the car by Tuesday. I'm sure all he cared about was getting to work. Nothing was about me.

"Rob, get up! You've got to take me to the hospital. I'm bleeding."

CHAPTER 13

The Gift Brings a Song

About two hours later, when the contractions were five minutes apart, we headed to the hospital. The anticipatory pain was just a dull ache. On arrival, the nurse examined me and informed me, I was four centimeters dilated. Attending a few sessions of Lamaze with Rob prepared me for what was to come. It was going to be a long wait. I didn't understand why I felt so comfortable. Where was all the drama attached to giving birth? When was the real pain going to start? Having heard so many stories, I figured the worst was yet to come. In the meantime, I smiled and chatted with the nurses amidst the screams of childbirth; quite relaxed and content. Not knowing how long we would have to wait, Rob decided to go home and take a shower.

"Please don't leave. What if the baby comes sooner than expected?"

"I won't be long," he said and left.

We lived about fifteen minutes away from the hospital. While Rob was gone, I was six centimeters dilated. At this point, the nurse enquired if I wanted an epidural. Still not experiencing any intense pain, I told her I didn't need it. She said firmly,

"My dear, if you don't have the epidural now, we won't be able to administer it later on."

"That's okay. I'll be fine," I answered, with certainty.

"How many children do you have?" she asked.

"This is my first child," I replied. She looked surprised.

"You're very brave. I thought you'd already been through childbirth." Smiling proudly and feeling kind of tough inside, I was ready.

When Rob returned, she suggested we take a few walks around the ward to see if it would induce labor. My waters had still not broken. I could feel the pain a tad sharper, but it was still very bearable. Nothing that would cause me to take a Tylenol.

Six hours in, the nurse examined me a third time. This time I was over eight centimeters dilated and my waters was still intact. That's when she suggested,

"We're going to have to break your water to induce labor. I'm calling your doctor to let him know you're ready." This didn't seem normal, but I didn't know enough to question her.

When Rob and I got to the delivery room, the lights were dimmed, and soft music played in the background. After I mounted onto the table, she informed me with a deliberately kind tone,

"Your doctor isn't available. Dr. Travis will be delivering your baby."

I didn't know who he was, and realized there was nothing I could do at that moment; the baby was coming, with or without my doctor. I felt a snap and gush as the nurse broke my water bag. It was about 3:00 p.m. Here it was; the pain I had heard about. Its intensity reached an almost numbing sensation that felt like it was subsiding and yet gathering momentum at a ridiculously increasing speed. The next twenty minutes were unbelievably excruciating, with no sense of rationality or self-control. A mother remembers the childbirth experience long after it happens, even when her child is an adult. Every sensation and emotion is unforgettable.

On September 20, 1995, at 3:21 p.m., I gave birth to a precious gift of life, a fearfully and wonderfully created human being, my son, David. He was the biggest miracle I had witnessed in life. This exquisite creature, crying his lungs out, formed inside of me from a fertilized egg within the space of just under nine months. That to me was the awesome power of God Almighty. God's hands at work. When the nurse placed him in my arms, still somewhat messy, I looked at my son, and immediately a love so profoundly extravagant emerged from within me and attached itself to this tiny miracle. He was mine.

After discharge, it was customary in the Indian culture for daughters to stay with their parents for the first forty days. My parents were beyond ecstatic. My husband wasn't happy, but he had no option. Joy had been unleashed on our family as we celebrated the first grandchild. My mom was thrilled about taking care of David and me. She loved every moment. So did my dad. And I was completely dazzled. I couldn't believe I was a mother. A truly remarkable moment in time! Rob, on the other hand, had mixed emotions. He was happy about having a baby, but not happy about David and I living with my parents.

Every evening after work, he came straight to the flat, ate dinner, and spent time with us. Even though he only worked five minutes away from the flat, and home was ten minutes away, he didn't like the setup. Twenty-one days later, David was christened in church. A few days earlier, Rob said to me,

"After the christening, I want you and the baby to come home. You've been here too long. And make sure you don't tell your parents I told you so."

"But they will ask me why. I have to tell them you said so."

"I don't care what excuse you make," he said, ending the conversation.

When I told my parents, they were disappointed.

"Dad. Mom. After the Christening on Sunday, Rob wants David and I to go home. He's not happy with us being here for so long. He said it's inconvenient. Please don't ask him. He told me not to tell you."

Disappointed we would be leaving, they fully understood the dynamics of the relationship. They knew him very well by now. And so, after the Christening, David and I went home.

Rob carried David into the house for the first time, took him straight to the nursery, and left him in the cot. Following him, I picked David up and walked around his nursery, excited to show him all the colorful paintings and designs I had created for him. He obviously had no idea what his mother was saying. Holding him in my arms, with his warm softness and the smell of Johnson's Baby Powder, made me feel like I belonged to him too. I was his Mommy.

Our rooms were adjoining. The nursery had two doors; one to our bedroom and the other to the dining room. The longer common wall between both bedrooms had a garden painted on it; a baby blue sky with a few fluffy white clouds. From the right corner, the sun peered across the garden. Along the skirting board, soft blades of green grass seemed to sway as though there was a gentle breeze. A tree with bright red apples stood in the middle of the garden, boasting colorful birds in flight among its branches. The scene had a natural beauty; just like my garden with Counselor.

On the opposite wall were cupboards from floor to ceiling, ending with the door leading into the dining room. Painted on one of the shorter walls were glittering silver stars and glow-in-the-dark planets. The opposite wall had a window with a little table. On it stood a lampshade, and a portable cassette player. The cot was placed against the garden scene with dangling soft, colorful toys suspended from the ceiling.

For the next three months, I stayed home and spent every waking moment with David. The Academy was a well-oiled machine and ran successfully without me during my maternity leave. Counselor always gave me a reason to live vicariously. Whether it was through our conversations or leading me to become a better version of myself, by discovering my gifts or reimagining my present and future. David was the focus of my love and human happiness, someone to hold and touch in the flesh. Every day my life got better and better. Now I had Counselor, David, Ama, caring family members and friends, and a thriving music business. I felt fulfilled.

Ever since I was a child, I would sometimes lose my sense of direction at any given time or place. Not once did I stop to think whether it was normal or not. When I lived with my parents, I didn't give it any consideration; they were always around. When I got married, I unknowingly depended on Rob's sense of direction since he drove all the time. During one of our conversations, it came up unintentionally. We were in the mall, and I said,

"I don't know where we are. Which way do we have to go?"

"What do you mean? You know the way. We've been here a hundred times before." That's when it hit me; I was different.

I explained to him how often this happened to me. I guessed that it started after I was molested. Explaining this odd phenomenon to him was unusual for me. I had never described it to anyone before that moment. So, I did my best to explain it to him.

"Sometimes, as I'm walking, I lose my sense of direction. I know where I am, but don't know how to get to the next point. For example, I know which mall we are in, but suddenly everything around me is unfamiliar. I know there are certain stores in the mall, but I don't know how to get to it, even though I'd been there before."

Saying nothing, Rob looked at me as if I was talking gibberish. I didn't blame him. This wasn't normal for him. How could he understand? Instead of continuing with something so nonsensical, I dropped the topic. This weird kind of memory loss did not impede my productivity or success. It momentarily affected my spatial sense. For the first time, I knew how different I was, and totally accepted this uniqueness without any questions or concerns. It never bothered me, until David came into my life.

Having saved enough money for a down payment on a new car, I decided it was time to buy myself a car, and drive it off the lot since I was a licensed driver. I didn't ask Rob for permission to purchase. On the contrary, I informed him and asked him if he could drive me to the dealer. He had no option. He also had no guilt or shame about taking over the first car I bought, and conveniently declaring it as his own. Not once did he apologize or offer some type of explanation. He didn't care. Outside of his control, I became the owner of a brand new Honda Ballade.

Immediately, I installed a baby car seat for David. It made it easier once I returned to work. Dropping David off at my parents' place, and then walking to work became a daily routine. I took a two-day position at a private school as a Music Specialist for a few hours to gain experience and exposure in hopes of expanding my business. It was about a forty-five-minute drive and a great opportunity to get comfortable on the road and gain some independence.

One particular day stands out. David was about age three, and I had to drop him off at Wonderland Preschool, a few blocks from home. Strapping him in his car seat, I got in the driver's seat, and drove to the first set of traffic lights. That's when this frightening thing happened; I lost my sense of direction. Up until then, I had accepted it for whatever it was. I didn't care to address it because it didn't have any negative impact on my life. In the car with me, was the littlest man who looked at his mommy with adorable bright almond-shaped eyes that said, *I totally depend on you, Mommy.*

I didn't hear those words, but I read them in the innocence of his face. I knew I had to do something about my condition. That evening when Rob got home, I told him what had happened.

"I need to see a psychologist. I have to know what this is and how I can rectify it."

"Do whatever you think you need to do," he said in a pleasantly supportive way.

That week I was in the psychologist's office. After telling him about my condition, he asked me to talk about my childhood. While I was relating my story to him, his eyes had a faraway look. I couldn't believe it. Here I was paying him a load of money to help my predicament, and he was daydreaming. He hadn't heard a word I had said. At the end of the session, instead of telling him what I really thought, I said,

"Thank you. I'm not sure if I need to have more sessions. I'll let you know."

He made no effort to convince me otherwise. One thing was certain; I wasn't going back to him. My kindness got the better of me; instead of saying something, I paid him for doing nothing. It was the same old Chloe who couldn't offend anyone, even if it cost me.

The second psychologist was a woman. The first thing I asked both doctors was this: "Do you know me from anywhere?"

That mattered to me because most people knew my face or my name. I played piano at one of the largest churches in Durban, and I owned the only Academy of its kind in the city. I had a reputation to uphold. I didn't want people thinking I was some nut case visiting a psychologist. There was a stigma attached to anyone who had to see a Mental Health physician. Her response was, "No."

Not having a reason to doubt her credibility, I went down the same path as the previous psychologist. However, this time, she stopped me midway and said,

"Chloe, I'm going to have to stop you. I didn't realize you were going to talk about such intense issues. I have to admit that I do know you and your family. Truth be told, I go to the same church as you do. In fact, you know my husband very well," and she went on to say his name, Gary.

Shocked at her admittance, I sat there dumbfounded.

"I'll understand if you choose to see another psychologist. I apologize for not stopping you earlier in the session."

How could this be? Of all the doctors in the city, I had to come to this one. Having shared the darkest parts of my life with her already, except for my married life, there was no use looking for someone else. I thought to myself, *Well, she did admit to her identity. That counts for something.*

And so, I agreed to continue sessions, and I'm glad I did. After two sessions, she said something to me that was transformative and life-changing.

"Chloe, when you were a child, the trauma was so intense that your brain found a way to help you survive. During stressful times or whenever you're anxious, your brain has learned how to shut off. It's like your brain goes on a break. That's how you've been dealing with the trauma. When you lose your sense of direction, that is really what's happening. Your brain forces you to forget."

"But how do I deal with this issue going forward? I can't afford my brain to forget anymore. I now have a child who depends on me. How do I handle being alone with him when we're not home?"

I couldn't tell her about Counselor in case she thought I was crazy. So, I kept him inside my heart.

"Whenever it happens, and you're alone with him, do you get more anxious?"

"Yes, I do. It worsens as soon as that happens."

"The next time it happens, try to relax and take a few deep breaths. When you do that, you'll get your spatial sense back. What you're really doing is tricking your brain by sending signals that you're not stressed. So, your brain will think there's no need to take a break. But when you get more anxious, your brain will stay in a shutdown mode until you're ready to deal with the matter at hand."

Whatever she said made total sense. The next thing would be for me to put it in action when it happened again. Hopeful and inspired, I thought about Counselor and my promise to him, *When I grow up, I want to be a Counselor just like you.*

I was in a very pensive frame of mind when I got home that evening. It was time to follow my next dream which simply put was following in Counselor's footsteps. I began researching graduate programs that would fit with my busy work schedule. That's when I stumbled across a great blended program, partly in-person and partly remote. It was the perfect fit for my lifestyle, and so I enrolled.

Finally, a lifelong dream was manifesting in real life. My world with Counselor had primed me for bigger and better things in life. I wished I could help people with their challenges by helping them find solutions. I wanted to give people what Counselor gave me - hope and a will to live in the midst of the storms in life, a way to rise above every situation no matter how dismal things looked, and the gift to believe that anything is possible if only we can imagine it.

Life is sometimes hard, but we choose the kind of life we want to live. Riches, fame, glamor, and success can't buy happiness. It's fleeting. Being content and living a life with purpose and meaning goes way beyond society's measurement of success. The code we humans live by is determined by the validation of others, rather than what comes from within. The day we stop trying to get people to like us, or we stop trying to impress people, is the day we give ourselves permission to look inside and see who we really are. We can't see the truth about ourselves when we keep looking at ourselves through the lens others have put on us. As a result, we have an unconscious bias towards ourselves. We continue to sabotage the better life we deserve. We judge ourselves according to opinions of others instead of setting our own moral compass. We must respect ourselves first, and then respect everyone else with fairness.

These are lessons Counselor taught me. To listen with my heart and my head. To step outside myself when listening to others and accept every story as valid, whether I agreed with it or not. Not to force my viewpoints or thoughts on others, but to help others see the best in themselves. This is the code I've been taught to live by, the code of deep understanding.

Life is hard. The rules are always changing. The players are always switching seats. But we get to play the game of life not like the game of chess, but as the game of hearts. Every person on the planet has experienced a broken heart or some type of disappointment or disillusionment. For when a heart is broken, it may take a lifetime to heal. Some hearts heal quicker than others, and some hearts never heal through their lifetime. Those broken hearts have turned hard, living to inflict pain on others. I sometimes imagine the torture in their minds and wish I could help them heal from their brokenness, so the world doesn't have to suffer at their hands. Life is hard, but we get to choose the kind of life we want. My heart healed in the garden with Counselor. This is what I want to share with the world. This is my purpose in life. This is what makes my life meaningful.

Sitting at the piano, I began writing songs and composing music again. The garden of my heart was being watered by creativity and life. David became my inspiration as I sat at my piano and composed the tenderness in a melody, dedicated to him. Every day, the music inside of me pulled me deeper. It was waiting to burst forth whenever I placed my hands on the keys. Songs flowed one after another. It was time to share some of my music with the world. I'd always wanted to do a concert tour, so I suggested to Rob,

"What do you think about going to the United States on a concert tour for about a month?" Rob loved challenge and adventure. This was right up his alley.

"That's a great idea. What do you have in mind?"

"Well, I was thinking of putting a group together. Maybe a couple of really talented students from the Academy and probably one or two musicians I've played with." He seemed to like the idea. Following his cue, I went on,

"Dad is connected to quite a few churches in the States. We could ask him to help set things in motion for us, then we can take it from there."

We pitched the idea to my dad, who was ready to jump on board with our plan. He made a few calls, and the rest was up to us. Between Rob and I, we coordinated about twenty concerts in total. The next step was for me to identify two students who I thought would complement each other and sound good together. Reaching out to their parents, since I had great relationships with them, I shared my vision. They were excited for their teenagers to be part of this fantastic adventure. Lastly, I approached one of the best bass guitarists in Durban and asked him if he was interested in coming along. Having never visited the States, he was eager to come along.

It was time to carefully comprise a repertoire. Understanding the American culture and what people enjoyed, I put together a mixed playlist; half original compositions with an African flavor and the other half were well-known songs.

It was a sensational tour, traveling with young musicians who oozed enthusiasm. Every place where we performed, people loved the sounds from Africa. It was different. It was vibrant. It was entertaining. Americans were mesmerized by the rhythms and harmonies of South Africa. They even loved our accent and wanted us to keep talking. For the performing artists in the group, it was an opportunity of a lifetime. An unforgettable experience!

When we returned home to South Africa, I asked Rob if Ama could come and live with us.

"She doesn't have a home. She goes from child to child, a few months at each place. Please, let's bring her here. We have three bedrooms. At least she doesn't have to live out of her suitcase all the time. Most of the time she won't even be here because she'll be with one of her children. This way, she has somewhere she can call home."

"You know I don't like people in my house. This will make it very awkward and uncomfortable for me."

"But she'll hardly be here. Just a few days here and there. Please." I asked, almost begging him to agree.

"Well okay. But as long as she doesn't get in my way. As soon as I feel she's crowding me, then she'll have to leave." Those were his conditions.

There was no way he would ask Ama to leave the house. She was already in her eighties. No one could be that cruel, not even Rob. So, I asked Ama to come and live with us. At first, she was dubious because of Rob, but I convinced her to stay.

"He said it is okay for you to stay with us," I told her as I held her feeble hands.

When she agreed, I was over the moon. At last, she will have some place to call her own. A few days later, she moved in. I helped her to unpack the old suitcase that she carried wherever she stayed. The both of us neatly packed all her clothing in the wardrobe, either on the shelves or on hangers. Inside my heart, I was crying out of compassion. At last, Ama has her own wardrobe in her private room.

"Ama, when you go to stay with your children, leave this big suitcase here. I have many small overnight bags. You can use one of those, whichever one you prefer. And if you need anything at any time, tell me, and I'll bring it to you." Ama, with her petite frame, embraced and kissed me.

"Thank you, my darling! God bless you."

Then she broke out into one of her sweetest songs as I lay my head on her tiny, frail shoulders. To me, she was still my city of refuge, the only place that held me safe, except for Counselor.

CHAPTER 14
Death and Dying

Every year we went away for a week's vacation, using our timeshare. When the house was being fumigated for wood bore, we decided to make a holiday out of it. No one was allowed on the property, so we checked Bentley and Belle into kennels close by. Being separated from them wasn't easy; we missed them tremendously. At the end of our vacation when we picked them up, imagine the excitement in the car on the way home. All five of us celebrated our reunion. Belle didn't leave my side while David was falling all over Bentley. He loved riding him like a horse; Thank God, Bentley was patient with him. He looked like a cuddly tricolored bear, enormous in size and gentle in spirit. His bark was bigger than his bite.

The next morning around 7 a.m., Rob left to work. He was in the garage when I heard his voice,

"Bentley my boy! What happened to you?"

I was still in bed. Something in my heart dropped. A bad feeling entered the pit of my stomach. Jumping out of bed, I threw on a gown and ran outside to the garage. Rob was bending over Bentley who lay still and cold.

"What happened to Bentley?" I cried out.

Rob didn't answer and just looked at me. I burst out crying. The ache inside my heart was unbearable. How did this happen? I canceled all my lessons and meetings for the next few days. I was inconsolable. I didn't expect this to happen. Bentley was only ten years old. He still had a few years left. We figured some of the poison must have been sprayed in his water bowl. There was no other explanation. He left such a huge gap in our lives. We missed him so much. David missed him too; it made him very sad.

I couldn't get over it for weeks. Rob suggested we get another dog. No one could replace Bentley, but we knew dogs have an intuitive power to help humans heal. That's when Benji came into our lives; a cross between a Labrador and a Siberian Husky. He was still a baby when we got him, but Belle made sure she trained him well. She still ruled the kingdom.

Ama came home after being away for about two months. I always felt surrounded by extreme love when she was around. While I studied, she sat with me. When I played the piano, she sat patiently listening to tunes I was working on. Often, I would study when David was asleep, until past midnight. It was the only time of uninterrupted silence.

Ama sat in the living room quietly, either listening to me play or waiting for me to finish whatever I was doing.

"Ama, you don't have to wait up for me. Go and sleep. I'll be fine." But she didn't budge.

"I want to be here with you, so you aren't alone. I'll wait for you. Don't worry about me. You carry on doing your work." Her nature was caring.

She felt indebted to Rob for allowing her to stay in our house. Because she was a nurturer at heart, she was always checking on him,

"Rob, can I get you anything?"

"Rob, how is your work?"

"Rob, why don't you eat? You must be hungry." This aggravated Rob. He felt she was crowding his space. One day he said to me,

"I've had enough. You have to ask your grandmother to leave. I can't be myself in my own house."

"But she's old. She has nowhere to go. How can I ask her to leave?"

"She's lived all her life without a home. She'll manage," he said without feeling.

"How cruel can he be," I thought?

I didn't know how I was going to tell her, but I had to. Otherwise, Rob would end up saying something hurtful to her, and I didn't want that to happen. The next day I had to break my Ama's heart.

"Ama, I have to tell you something that isn't easy for me," I started.

"I know Ma, I know," she said. Ma was a loving way to address someone dear to one's heart in the Indian culture. Looking at her curiously, I asked her,

"What do you know, Ama?"

"Rob doesn't want me to stay here."

I didn't know if she heard him say so or if she intuitively picked it up. But she knew. I helped her pack her clothes with a huge lump in my throat and anger in my heart. What I didn't do to save my marriage, and to please my husband, at the expense of everyone else including myself?

Jonathan had just returned from a two-week trip to Cape Town, a city on the west coast of South Africa, the home of Robben Island. This is where Nelson Mandela had been imprisoned for eighteen years in solitary confinement. Although he was visiting Simon, I wondered if there was a hidden message lurking in the solitude and separation, hovering over Robben Island. Something seemed amiss, but I just couldn't put my finger on it. I was at unrest, and I couldn't shake it off.

As soon as he got back to Durban, he called me immediately. Excited to hear his voice, I readily accepted his invitation to dinner that same night. The fact is, Jonathan wasn't just my younger brother, we were best friends. At my wedding, that's precisely what he said in his speech, "Chloe is not just my sister. She's my best friend."

"Howzit?" he asked, using a South African greeting between close family and friends meaning, "Hello. How are you?"

"Chloe, I've asked dad and mom to come over for dinner. And I'm also going to invite Charlee and her husband over. Please come over for a family dinner. We all haven't seen each other in so many weeks."

That was so typical of Jonathan; always making an effort to bring the family together. Without hesitation I said,

"Sure. I'd love to. When Rob gets home from work, I'll tell him. We'll come over after he changes into casual clothes."

Around 6 p.m., Rob walked through the door. I happily shared the evening plans, not suspecting any kickback. He observed my excitement and knew how close Jonathan and I were.

"As soon as you settle in and change, we can leave," I said in a contented manner to which he point-blankly said, "No," without reason or further comment.

"I didn't make dinner because I thought we were going to Jonathan's place," I said.

"Well, we're not going, so go into the kitchen and cook something," he shot back sharply, shutting me down.

If I continued the conversation, I knew it would worsen. Surrendering, I let it slide instead of setting myself up for a fall. If only I'd understood the ambiguity around the fall, earlier than later, I may have persevered.

Walking to the bedroom, frustrated and sad in the same breath, I picked up the phone to call Jonathan. He was far from happy when he heard my sorry excuse,

"Hey, I'm not going to make it tonight. I have a tummy ache."

He wasn't convinced because he knew me too well. He probably saw right through the pretense. Jonathan suggested we visit for a short while, but I didn't budge. I couldn't. I lied to protect my husband from developing a reputational scar with my family. That wasn't the only reason. Listening in on the whole conversation, he was waiting to pounce, waiting for one word of error. From Jonathan's tone, I could tell he was upset. He probably knew I wasn't telling the truth and he must have guessed that Rob was right there next to me. After his attempt to persuade me, Jonathan realized there was nothing he could say to change my answer. Giving up, he said, "Goodbye," and we ended the call.

Jonathan and I hadn't spoken for almost two weeks after that, causing the dull void in my heart to echo dimly. Lying to him, about why I couldn't see him, wedged an unwelcome separation in our closeness. He didn't understand my lame excuse because the reason lacked rationality, aside from the fact, it was out of character for me. How could it make sense to him when it didn't even make sense to me? What started as a straightforward story, complicated itself within a matter of minutes.

For the next two weeks, there was no communication. That was the first time we hadn't spoken for such an extended period. Jonathan didn't call not only because he was upset with me, but he was busy with work as well. When he saw me in church, he intentionally looked the other way. Deep down in my heart, I knew he found it hard to understand why I had lied. He was probably more upset that I didn't trust him enough to tell him what was really wrong. I wish I had found a way to tell him the truth before it was too late. As for Rob and me, we defaulted to the 'no-communication' zone. I felt anger rise up toward him but didn't have the courage to act upon it or say anything in my defense.

The weather forecast didn't deliver promising news for the weekend. I dragged myself out of bed on the dull, dreary morning of Saturday, August 8, 1998, and headed to the video rental store. A few months prior, the movie *Titanic* showed at all the movie theaters in South Africa. Having thoroughly enjoyed it, I thought it would be a great idea to watch it again. It was a good day for a movie and popcorn. At least I would be entertained for a little over three hours, snuggled under the covers while David happily played with his toys.

It rained most of the day, with low temperatures. Before jumping into my car to drive to the video rental store, the phone rang. When I picked it up, Jonathan was on the other end. He was at the church building, picking up the car he had parked overnight in the church garage. Noticing one of the students waiting outside the Academy, he was concerned. The area was usually deserted on Saturdays. It wasn't safe for students to be hanging around on their own. There was always the potential danger because of the high crime rate in the city of Durban.

After two weeks of silence, Jonathan and I spoke for about five minutes that morning. Most of the conversation was casual chitchat. What a relief to break the unnecessary tension that was created! My mind was at peace. The ice had been broken. By the end of the day, I was sure we would be back to normal, catching up on the phone. I couldn't wait to tell him what really happened on that awful night.

I was fifty-five minutes into the movie when the phone rang again. This time, Rob picked up the phone, "Hello."

I could hear screaming on the other end. My guts felt like it was imploding on the inside. It kept sending me messages I refused to accept. Somehow, I knew something terrible had happened. It felt like a cold hand had recklessly plunged itself into my ribcage, squeezing every drop of life out of my heart. My world came to a standstill. When the call ended, Rob calmly said,

"I'm going to take a drive to your parents' flat to see what's going on."

He actually wanted to leave me at home, knowing what he knew. This was my family. My brother. Not his. My brother. His audacious suggestion angered me. I firmly put down my foot, and insisted,

"No. You're not. David and I are coming with you."

Distraught, I rushed around throwing on some warm clothes; first on David then myself.

When we got to my parents' place, my sister Charlee opened the door, screaming repetitively, "Jonathan's gone,"

A moment later, Jonathan's wife came running behind her, frantically screaming utter nonsensical words that were totally distorted. Without any feeling or sympathy, I looked at them and said,

"Would you both stop talking nonsense? Pull yourselves together!"

I pushed past them and made my way to my parents' bedroom. My father and mother sat on their bed in a stupor.

"What's wrong with you all? There's nothing's wrong with Jonathan. It's a mistake, can't you see?"

I desperately and deniably convinced myself that the footage of the car accident flashing across the television screen wasn't Jonathan's car going up in flames. I refused to believe their lie. For me, it was a complete lie.

Rob and my sister's husband went to the mortuary to identify the so-called body.

Let them go. They will see it isn't Jonathan, I tried to convince myself.

In the meantime, Simon was on a flight from Cape Town. People were pouring into my parents' home, all day and all night long, offering their condolences with stunned and shocked expressions. Emotionless, I stood like a statue not shedding a single tear. I couldn't cry. I couldn't pretend to cry. No tears were falling from my eyes. I couldn't even mimic empty sobs. Jonathan would never have left without saying goodbye. Things weren't fully restored between us. Our story was incomplete. He would have waited for me.

At that moment, Rob came towards me and took me in his arms to comfort me. Although I allowed him to, I felt intense hatred toward him. He was the reason Jonathan and I hadn't spoken. I couldn't believe this was really happening. Yet I didn't say a word, and I didn't shed a tear.

Later in the evening, Simon walked through the door, and for the first time, the truth finally hit me. I began to howl, realizing Jonathan wasn't coming back and we'll never be fully restored again. I wanted to cry out to Jonathan and say, "Please wait for me. We're not done." But he couldn't hear me anymore.

It was over. Jonathan was gone, and my heart continued to beat like a dull, dead drum. How was I to know our last conversation would mark one of the final exchanges between brother and sister as well as best friends? Jonathan was gone, and I never got to tell him how much I loved him.

Three weeks later, I experienced my first birthday without Jonathan. He always coordinated my birthday dinners and made it so special for me. To him, seeing me smile, made his day. I promised myself I would never celebrate my birthday again because Jonathan wasn't with me anymore.

That night, I cried myself into a sleepless night. "Jonathan, wherever you are, please know how much I love you. I miss you. Please forgive me."

There was bitterness in my heart toward Rob. I blamed him, but I never dared say anything to him. We continued living together. We kept pretending. We portrayed ourselves as a power couple. We never showed the world outside what life was like on the inside. What lay behind closed doors stayed behind closed doors. The mattress I lay on had thorns and roses. After a while, the pain from the piercing of a thorn, transformed into numbness. The more the thorns, the more desensitized I became to the thorns. Counselor had shown me how to breathe in the absence of oxygen. I learned that things in life were counterintuitive. As humans, we want to make sense of life, but more often than not, life doesn't make sense. Life happens to us regardless if we want it to or not. Life comes knocking at our door and frequently enters without our permission. The strong at heart learn how to climb mountains and cross great divides in the marathon of life.

In life, there are certainties and uncertainties. Every human being experiences life in this way. One of those uncertainties is death. We never know when we'll take our last breath. Death comes to every species of life. No one is exempt. How we choose to live life depends on us. I blamed Rob for many things, but realistically speaking I had choices. I wasn't courageous enough to take the risk and speak up despite what Counselor told me, "Only you can say the words."

I believed the voice of the Counselor and Coach in my heart and in my head. The inner critic within us will always scream for attention. But there is also a friend inside each one of us that values and sees us. It was time for the real me to emerge. Believing the voice was one thing. Acting on it was something entirely different. I had to find the courage to challenge. I had to speak up and speak out. I had to say something. I knew it would be a process and that these things don't happen overnight.

In my hand, I held a certificate with my name on it. My dream to be a Counselor had finally become a reality. I graduated with my Master's degree in Christian Counseling. It may have been a mighty long haul, but worth the while. My experiential education started way before I enrolled in the program. At age nine, I met someone who changed my life forever. Now was the time to pay it forward. My chance to help others see the beauty and worth within themselves; this was the reason I was born. One thing is certain; life happens to every single person on the face of the earth, and I wanted to be part of the grand design of as many lives as possible. I wanted to teach people how to access the friend inside of them, instead of giving voice to the inner critic. I wanted to see people embrace a better version of themselves. I wanted to see love and compassion spread across the face of this earth.

Just when I thought, the story of death and dying had ended its season in our lives, something unexpected happened. Rob's mother, a vibrant woman, physically active and very involved with church activities, had suddenly taken ill. Without warning, she collapsed at her home and was taken to the hospital, unaware she had suffered a heart attack. We expected her to recover within a few days. On the Sunday after church, we visited her at the hospital. Her husband, Rob and his sister, and I were present. His mom looked at me and said, "Come closer to me, Chloe."

Moving closer, so I was right next to her, she held my hand and shared a vision she had seen the previous night.

"I saw Jesus standing at the foot of the bed. He kept calling me to come to him. What do you think that means?"

I knew it was her time, but I couldn't say that to her. Nor could I say it to the rest of the family members. I kept it in my heart. Her eyes never left me, as she waited for my response.

"It means that Jesus is with you. He's watching over you," I said while squeezing her hand gently as a sign of comfort.

When it was time to go, she asked me to pray over her. I prayed for peace in her heart and in her mind. The next day I wasn't able to go. In the early parts of the following morning, the hospital called to say she had taken a turn for the worse. Rob got dressed and rushed to the hospital. She passed away before he reached there.

I distinctly remember what she said to me on the day Jonathan had passed. It was just a few months earlier.

"Chloe, he can't come back to us, but we can go to where he is."

I never thought she would be the first one to go to where Jonathan is.

We are faced with uncertainties every day. Life is filled with opportunities that have the potential to bring us joy or teach us something about ourselves. We get to live our lives once. Being fully alive in every moment is a gift because every moment only lasts a split second. When that moment has passed, no matter what we do, we can never get it back again. If we don't intentionally make wise decisions, we miss out on opportunities to experience how phenomenal we can be. We create our memories. We don't get a do-over in life. We do life!

CHAPTER 15
Goodbye South Africa, Hello USA

After Jonathan's death, I felt a restlessness in my spirit as the winds of change were blowing. Everything I did began to inspire me less and less. Some things had changed. The Academy was running too smoothly and successfully. It had become somewhat mundane. Leading the music and worship in church felt too ordinary. I needed something more. Now that I had completed my degree in Counseling, I started to think of what was next for me. I knew I didn't want to just be a board-certified Counselor. What I needed was something different, something exciting! Having established a name for myself in the city as a performing artist, motivational speaker, leadership consultant and businesswoman, I was positioned for something bigger. There was a deep stirring inside my heart. At that moment, I had a flashback of something Counselor said to me,

"Inside your heart, resides the whole world."

The living map hanging on the wall of the Grace Room in my heart began to light up. My heart was beaming. This was it! Time for launch! Something! Somewhere! Somehow!

My parents were invited to an exclusive dinner with a group of pastors. Investors from the United States were guests at the event. At the end of the dinner, my mother, a hospitable woman who was also an excellent cook, invited four of the guests for a traditional Durban Indian home-cooked meal. Whenever she had guests over, she always invited Rob and me. Not having any expectations at all, we joined them. It was a pleasant evening with great conversation. Before we bid farewell, business cards were exchanged. Rob was kind enough to help them with certain business matters, and they were appreciative.

A few months later, we received an email from one of the gentlemen. He made us an offer to come to the United States on a contract basis for six months. He offered both Rob and me paid leadership positions. He needed assistance in community development projects and its administration, predominantly in the low-income African American community in South Central Los Angeles. We had no idea where that was located. To us, Los Angeles was LA, and LA was Hollywood. As South Africans, we didn't know the difference. Just like when Americans had asked me about lions roaming the streets of South Africa when I was in Rochester. In addition to his offer, we would also represent South Africa in the broader HIV/Aids initiative he was involved in.

We told him we would give it some thought. Living thousands of miles away from family and the Durban Indian culture would be a dramatic change for the three of us.

Ama was ninety-two, and her health was declining rapidly. She had severe incontinence. Traveling weighed heavily on her, so she stayed with my mom for most of the time. On the other hand, my mom wasn't strong enough to take care of her. Ama's three children decided the best option was to find a good Care Facility. One of my cousins, a nurse at a well-maintained facility about thirty minutes from the city, managed to pull some strings and secure a room for Ama. It wasn't an easy decision. The day she was being checked into the facility, the whole family accompanied her. She was so unhappy. There was such sorrow in her eyes. She cried as she said,

"Please don't leave me here. I'll die here. I don't want to die with strangers."

But there was nothing anyone could do. It broke my heart. All of us were feeling sad with her. We all loved her tremendously. I wished I could have taken care of her, but it was impossible. My cousin assured us that special attention would be given to Ama. After we left her, I cried all the way home. That night, I couldn't sleep. All I could see was Ama's face. I stayed up the whole night praying for her, just like she always prayed for me. How could I leave Ama and go to the United States? What if anything happened to her?

Still waiting to see where life was going to take me, I decided to enroll in a Computer College to study Information Technology. I figured if computers were a thing of the future, I'd better learn something about it. Excited but feeling kind of old with twenty-year-old classmates, I didn't let it get me down. In fact, they enjoyed having me in the class. If I didn't understand something, they took the time to explain it to me. Within the first two months, I was able to assemble a whole computer and hook up a simple network. It gave me a rush! At my age in the year 2000, that was pretty cool for a woman. It was great being a student in college again. Every Monday through Thursday, I attended classes from 9 a.m. to 12 p.m. and I was becoming technologically savvy. Change was happening rapidly in all areas of my life. I still didn't know what my destination looked like. I waited in anticipation.

I had just finished class and was exiting the building, when I bumped into Jeff, an old high school friend. It was really great to see him and catch up after so many years. We stood and spoke in the reception area, while I waited for Rob to pick me up. When he asked for my cell number, I could feel fear rise up and choke me. Not wanting to create something out of nothing, I gave it to him. A week later, he called me. I had just finished class.

"Chloe, I'll be in town tomorrow. I'd love to connect with you if you're free."

"Sure," I said.

"I can meet you at the college around noon. Is that okay?"

"That's okay," I replied.

I don't know why I agreed. I didn't know how to say, "No. I can't meet you. If my husband found out, he would make my life a living hell."

Why did I think I was doing something wrong? This was an old friend, and we were hanging out for a few minutes in public. All the students were there. What could go wrong? When it came to Rob's suspicious mind anything was possible.

The next day, I met Jeff. It was refreshing being able to talk to someone openly. He said he usually came into the city about two or three times a month. We shared stories about our lives, our families, and our jobs. I said nothing about the real state of my marriage; I was too embarrassed to talk about it. Other students were around while we talked. It was pure and innocent.

After about thirty minutes, I told him I had to go. Rob called to say he couldn't pick me up; he was tied up in a meeting. So, I headed over to my parents' flat; a fifteen-minute walk. All the hype of guilt was for nothing.

As soon as I entered the flat, I breathed a sigh of relief. Being in the presence of my parents always brought a sense of ease to me. My dad said,

"Chloe, someone from the Care Facility called."

"Is Ama okay?" I asked with great concern.

"Yes. The nurse wanted to know who Chloe was. Ama keeps calling your name."

An ache punched me hard in the stomach. I couldn't bear to think she was alone spending the final years of her life with strangers. A sudden urge to see her overtook me. I decided we would visit her on the weekend.

When Saturday arrived, I cooked her a bland meal because her digestive system couldn't handle anything spicy, and took her a slice of fruit loaf, her favorite cake. When she saw David, Rob and me, she was absolutely thrilled. Her face lit up. Lifting her frail body with all the strength she could muster, she hugged us as tightly as her frailty allowed. I fed her, talked to her, rubbed her back, cut her nails, and prayed with her. David wanted to sit on the bed with her and comb her hair. She let him, and then cuddled with him. Ama's smile on her face was more than enough for me. It made my day.

Charlee had it on her heart for Ama to spend a whole day with us. I thought it was an excellent idea. She picked her up from the Care Facility one morning, and brought her over to my house. I made a spread for her; all her favorite foods but quite bland. David, Charlee and I spent the whole day, talking and showering her with tons of love and kisses. We really spoilt her and allowed her to spoil us too. By the middle of the afternoon, it was time for her to leave. Ama cried, refusing to go. We tried to persuade her as best we could, but she didn't want to listen to a word we were saying. Charlee and I didn't know what we were going to do. The only way was for Rob to carry her to the car. We cried as we witnessed our darling Ama fighting to stay with us. When she settled in the car, she sobbed uncontrollably. I grabbed her and told her how much I loved her. In my gut, I knew this was it.

A few weeks later, the Care Facility called to say she was in her final moments. All of us rushed to see her. She didn't recognize any of us as she stared at the ceiling with glassy eyes; a faraway look in her eyes. I called her name,

"Ama, it's Chloe." She turned and looked at me, then looked away, and said,

"I can see Jesus. I can see heaven." She closed her eyes, and slipped away into eternity.

My Ama was gone. My City of Refuge! I held her in my heart forever. I have never stopped calling her name at different times in my life. She may be gone to heaven, but her memory still lives in my heart. Counselor told me so many years ago,

"I've given you someone who loves you very much. If you look closely, you'll find that person." He was right. I found her. She was my Grace, and the room in my heart was named after her.

As if I had a greater capacity to take on more, Belle got sick and started to limp. This couldn't be happening. The restlessness of my heart was an indication of things to come. I was expecting happy things to happen, not less. That's when Counselor reminded me,

"Chloe, after death comes resurrection. For this season of your life, you're in the Dark Room. Remember what happens here?" It was difficult to think.

There was too much loss of life that was coming at me. Depending totally on Counselor to answer the question he asked, I said,

"Please remind me. I'm struggling to think through all the loss I'm experiencing."

"It's where you grow and develop. The darkness makes you develop faster than the light. A seed that's planted in the ground can only germinate in a dark place. Here's the miracle. A green shoot can only spring to life when the seed dies. And that's your name. Chloe means 'a green shoot.' It's your time to develop into a tree that grows in stature and strength. It gives life. It provides sustenance. It's the shade from the heat. That's what you've been created for. To give life and hope to all who cross paths with you."

I also remembered Counselor once saying to me that I could find a reason in everything that happens in life. But the process was too painful.

Belle began to slow down day by day. We took her to the vet who said,

"It's old age. She's lived a good life."

For seventeen years, she was my guardian angel and my protector. She was faithful and loving. She made me feel safe. I wasn't afraid when I was with her because I knew without a shadow of doubt she had my back. I reminisced about both Bentley and Belle sitting on the kitchen floor with David, Rob and I, their heads on our laps, utterly content. She was an amazing dog. She indeed ruled the kingdom. The vet told us,

"She has about three months left. Take her home and show her all the love you can. You'll know when her time is up." And that's what we did until her final breath.

Meanwhile, we got our answer. Every incident was a sign. It was time to move. We accepted the offer to relocate to Los Angeles. My parents were supportive of our decision, although my mom didn't like it. David and I would be too far away from her. We decided to share the news with our close friends and family. Everyone had mixed feelings. They were happy for us, but sad to see us go.

A few weeks later a horrific event took place that shook the world - 9/11. My God! When was it going to stop? I couldn't make it stop. No wonder there was a restlessness in my heart. The winds of change were not just blowing, they were howling. The first thing people asked us, "So, you guys are canceling your trip?"

And our answer remained the same, "No."

We were set to leave on December 30, 2001, a little over three months. This was enough time to spend with Belle, tie up things for the house, and complete my Diploma in Information Technology. The three-week course I completed in Microsoft Office sharpened my skills and taught me a few quick tricks. After persuading my dad, I offered to pay for him to attend classes. At least I got to hang out with him a few times a week. Jeff called me again to let me know he was going to be in town. Talking to someone unsupervised was nice. He made me feel special. We hung out in the College common room and chatted over coffee. When I told him that we were moving to the States, he said he'd like to stay in touch and asked for my email address. Not thinking anything of it, I gave it to him. I didn't know if I would be seeing him again, so we bid farewell and he hugged me.

A few days later, I received an email from him stating he had feelings for me. Fear shot up in me! I recognized it too well. Fear of opening up myself to something I didn't expect. Fear of Rob ever finding out about this whole thing.

Not knowing how to give him the brush off, I emailed back and told him how much I enjoyed our conversations, he was a good friend, but the both of us were married. Somewhere deep inside me was an aboding fear that I couldn't shake.

That evening, when Rob got home, he found the emails. I must have left them open by mistake. He was enraged, and insisted I was having an affair. This was the real X-Factor for me. I thought he was going to kill me. He kept saying it over and over again. He demanded an admission from me. He went on for hours until I was forced to answer,

"Yes," thinking that would set his mind straight, and quieten him. That was the worst thing I could have done. From that moment on, things started to spiral out of control. I couldn't take him anymore. He became extremely aggressive. He pushed death in my face, threatening me and calling me names. I thought to myself, *No wonder I looked forward to talking to Jeff.*

Nothing I said after that registered in Rob's head. He stopped me from attending any more classes. The next day, he went to the college and enquired about my classmates. I'm sure he threatened the office staff too. He had a way of drawing information out of people. There were twelve of us in the class. Assuming one of the twenty-year-old guys was Jeff, he accused him of having an affair with me and asked him to leave me alone. How embarrassing and humiliating!

To check on my assignments, I called one of my classmates, and she related this incident to me. I asked her if I could speak to the guy who Rob threatened. I wanted to apologize. As I was holding on, I heard him say,

"There's no way I'm not talking to her. Her husband is crazy."

Rob was stuck on my admission. I couldn't do anything to retract it. He believed it, and I lived through the interrogation every day. I apologized so many times, but he heard nothing. He made sure I was never out of his sight. He blamed my sister for influencing me and refused to let me speak to her. He stopped me from visiting my parents. It was already the second week of December, and we were leaving the country within the next three weeks. I didn't know when I would see them again. He insisted I leave David at the flat, so he could have me to himself.

Every night he made reckless love to me, punishing me and hurting me. He disregarded my cries of pain and hurt. He was the master teaching his servant how to be obedient. Counselor was right again. I was in the Dark Room. Something was developing in me. I didn't know what it was, but I knew that one day something beautiful would emerge. I was born for greater things, and I couldn't afford to be shortsighted. There was a reason to be found, and I searched for it with all my heart.

Chloe is a good girl. Chloe is a good girl. Chloe is a good girl. I repeated over and over again until I began to believe it. In a few weeks, we would be far away from the people I loved and cared for. I had to find my strength again. I had to rise up and live again. I had to learn to breathe again. I had to, for myself and for David.

David didn't want to accept that Belle was not going to be around for long. It was a hard time for him too; first Bentley went, then he had to say goodbye to his uncle who fondly called him Buster. A few months later his grandma passed away, then Ama who he adored was gone. And now, Belle. It was too much for his little mind to absorb so much loss in such a short space of time.

In a few weeks, he would be saying goodbye to his grandparents, and to everything that meant something to him. The day we said goodbye to Belle was just too painful. I had to keep reminding myself that I could find a reason for everything. All I had to do was look for the light in the darkness. I had to be strong again, for David and for myself.

With a mix of untold emotions, a range of unshared thoughts, the next chapter of our lives awaited us. The possibilities were limitless. The opportunities were endless. The road ahead seemed aimless, but I knew that bigger and better things waited for us at our destination.

Counselor told me that my imagination was a powerful tool. It can take me anywhere I want it to, in and out of danger and fear. You never know with life. Anything can happen if we believe.

In all the years I've lived, one life-changing revelation stands out for me as an anchor; the story we tell ourselves is the story we end up living. Bad things happen to good people all the time. And good things happen to bad people. There are certainties and uncertainties in life. There are constants and variables. Some things stay the same. Most things evolve and change. As human beings, we default to the inner critic inside of us. It's our negativity bias. This is the revelation that continues to keep me alive and living.

If there's an enemy inside of us, then there has to be a friend somewhere in there too. Be kind to yourself and find your inner friend because when we access the voice of the Counselor and the Coach within, we stand defiantly, speak courageously, listen intently - and we live magnificently

---

As the plane lifts off South African soil and heads for the tall trees and bushes of secluded area, it holds a compelling mystery to me. I behold the beauty of the forest and realize it's all part of my garden with the Big Red Heart. I close my eyes and slip into my beautiful world with Counselor.

"Are you ready Chloe?" he asks me.

"Yes, I am," I reply, smiling.

"I have a surprise waiting for you," he teases me lovingly, "You want to know what it is?"

"Of course, I want to know. Tell me."

"Come with me. I'll show you." He took me by the hand and we strolled through the garden towards the Big Red Heart.

"Go ahead, open the door," he says.

Placing both my hands on the Big Red Heart, I closed my eyes. Suddenly the gentle heartbeat I was accustomed to could no longer be heard. In its place was a new sound. It was different, thrilling, powerful, and forceful. My heart beat like the sound of horses' hooves, galloping with fierce velocity. It wasn't just one horse; it was an army of horses. I couldn't tell the difference between my heart and Counselor. It sounded like a symphony of rhythms, beats, sounds, and vibrations. We were inside the Big Red Heart in the grand hallway standing in front of the fourth door, an old rustic wooden door with thick iron bolts that aged back to thousands of years. Wondering what mystery lay behind the fourth door, I slowly and carefully lifted my trembling hands, placed them on the heavy bolt and pulled it back, to unlock the secrets within, waiting to be discovered.